# Organise Yourself

# *Organise Yourself*

## Ronni Eisenberg
with Kate Kelly

PIATKUS

*To Alan And George,*
*who helped keep*
*Julia, Amanda, and Elizabeth*
*'organised'*
*so that this book*
*could be written.*

First published in
Great Britain in 1988 by
Judy Piatkus (Publishers) Ltd.,
5 Windmill Street, London W.1

British Library Cataloguing in Publication Data

Eisenberg, Ronni
  Organise yourself.
  1. Executives——Time management
  I. Title II. Kelly, Kate
  658.4'093      HD38.2

  ISBN 0-86188-706-9
  ISBN 0-86188-718-2 Pbk

Typeset by Action Typesetting Limited, Gloucester
and printed in Great Britain by
Mackays of Chatham Ltd, Kent

# CONTENTS

# Section 4/Household Matters 91

# Section 5/Main Events 129

# Section 6/Personal Agenda 171

# Section 7/Children 203

# Index 227

# Introduction

Whenever I tell people what I do for a living — teaching others how to become better organised — the response is almost invariably, 'Boy, could I use you!' And they are basically right, because everyone can be better organised. Often that comment is followed by a sigh and a true confession: 'Organising takes too much time. I just can't be bothered.' Other familar statements I hear are:

- 'I don't know how!'
- 'It's easier to let things go!'
- 'I have children.' (!)
- 'If I get organised, I won't be creative any more.'
- 'My problems are different from those of everyone else (I get more post, I have more appointments, responsibilities, etc.), so I can't get organised.'
- 'Getting organised will be too predictable and boring.'

While people may believe these excuses are true, the fact remains that you probably 'won't be famous if you don't know where things are . . .'

People who are successful share a common secret. They know that to get ahead, they must plan, set priorities, and always follow through. As a result they develop systems that work for them. Their reward? Peace of mind and a gift of extra time — no more looking for the missing file folder, the other sock, or a friend's telephone number. (It's frightening to imagine the hours *wasted* on disorganisation!)

*Organisation is being able to find what you're looking for — getting things done — being in control of your life.* Why spend time looking for your keys when you could be locking the door and going out to have a good time?

With most people, I find that there comes a time when they simply have to face the fact that because of disorganisation, their lives aren't working for them. For one client things got so bad she had to move out of her flat; another came to me because she couldn't stand having her cheques bounce any more;

a third telephoned saying her desk 'looked like an archaeological dig, there were so many levels of civilisation to uncover . . .'; a fourth called after she bought a new evening dress and shoes and had her hair done for a black tie event − only to go on the wrong night. One called immediately after he had seen my name in the newspaper. I was impressed with his efficiency until he said, 'I was afraid that if I didn't call you now, I would lose the little scrap of paper I've written your number on.' The list goes on and on.

I recently met a woman who said, 'You know, my life would be so simple, if only I were organized. I'm so disorganised that I go to the supermarket and forget why I'm there. I get to a meeting, and I've left the papers I needed behind; I'm always late . . .'

'Why do you avoid getting organised?' I asked her.

'I just don't know,' was her reply.

You've bought this book, so you must have decided that − for you − *now* is the time to learn how to get organised. And I've got good news for you: organisation is a skill; it *can* be learned. The most difficult part is breaking those lifelong bad habits (like letting your paperwork pile up). Anybody can get organised if they want to badly enough. Just start with one small step and then take others, one at a time. Once you see the benefits in one part of your life, you will be motivated to go on!

If you implement the ideas given here, you'll be free from chaos and able to control your life instead of having *it* control you.

Just do me one favour. Once you've started, stick with the recommended organisational process. Getting organised is the first step; persistence and follow-through are the keys to staying that way.

The process of getting organised will amaze you. You may find that what you've been putting off for years takes only an hour to do! Believe me, it takes *less* time to be organised − it's actually *easier* to be organised − so get started!

# Section 1
~
# Getting Control of Your Time

# 1: Procrastination

Are you a procrastinator? Here are some warning signs:

- Do you often wait until the last minute to start a project?
- Do you frequently send belated birthday cards?
- Do you do all your Christmas shopping on Christmas Eve?
- Do you regularly put off going to the doctor or dentist?
- How long have you been waiting to clean out your cupboard/drawers/kitchen/medicine cabinet?
- Do you often put off making a decision about something?
- Are you waiting for the 'right' time to make that dreaded phone call, confront your boss about a well-deserved rise, or start an exercise programme?
- Did you leave this chapter until last?

Most of us procrastinate in one area or another. Some people procrastinate about everything. It's only natural. As children, we learned that procrastination brought a certain element of satisfaction. If we delayed something (like Mum's request that we clean our room), we at least gained some control over the task; we had to do it, but at least *we* said when. That's important to a child who has so little say over most things. What's more, if we procrastinated long enough, we learned that someone (good old Mum) might sometimes do it for us — and that was worth waiting for!

As adults, procrastination generally signals some type of internal conflict. While we've made the decision to do something, there's still a part of us that holds back. Some of the reasons people procrastinate are the following:

- *They feel overwhelmed.* This usually happens when there is an overload of information or too many details.
- *They overestimate the time needed.* They think the task is too time-consuming, that it will take *for ever*. A variation of this is thinking that they have for ever to finish something.

- *They'd rather be doing something else.* Anything seems better than what awaits them.
- *They think that if they wait long enough, it will go away.* The project will be cancelled; the appointment postponed, and so forth.
- *They want to do it perfectly.* People often fear turning in a report or finishing a project because they worry about failing on 'judgement day'. They delay until the last minute, and then if it doesn't measure up, they say, 'Oh, I would have done better if I'd had more time.'
- *They don't want to assume responsibility.* After all, if they never complete the project, no one will hold them responsible.
- *They fear success.* If they complete something and succeed, will they be able to continue to live up to that standard? How will others relate to them once they are successful?
- *They say they enjoy the last-minute adrenalin rush.* Often people feel that they do their best work 'under pressure'. What they fail to remember are the times when they had a terrible cold or there was a family emergency during the time they had intended to devote to the project.

## *Identifying your reasons for procrastinating*

- First you must determine which situations generally cause you to procrastinate. Consider the following questions:
  - ★In what types of situation do you usually procrastinate?
  - ★How has it worked against you?
  - ★What price did you pay for the delay?
  - ★When you have procrastinated for a long time and then finally do it, what finally gets you going? (Imminent deadline? Reward? Some outside pressure?)
- When you find yourself procrastinating about something specific, consider the following:
  - ★What about this situation causes conflict for you? What are you avoiding?
  - ★If you delay, what is likely to be the result?
  - ★If the question really is *when* to do it (and there is really no possibility that you won't do it), ask yourself if you truly want to pay the price of a delay.

# *27 ways to stop procrastinating*

- The hardest part is getting started. Once you're in motion, it will be easier to stick with it. You may well find that it isn't as bad as you expected, and once you're *involved,* you've overcome the biggest hurdle.

- Procrastinators often have an unrealistic sense of time; you may have the feeling that a project will take *for ever* or that you have 'plenty of time'. The more realistic you become, the less likely you'll be to procrastinate. To get a better sense of time, start keeping a log of how long various projects take. (Use your desk diary to keep track. You can do a tally at the end of each month.) How long did you *really* spend making those personal calls? Only one hour? That wasn't so bad. How long did it take to pack for a family holiday? How much time did you spend doing your family budget?

- Work with the time available to you. Sometimes people estimate that a project will take 10 or 12 hours, so they keep waiting for a day when they can devote that amount of time to it. Of course, that day never comes. Break the project down into small, manageable parts. This is your insurance against procrastination. List each step you need to take in order to complete a task. For example, if you're planning a household move, begin by researching which company to use. Ask friends for recommendations, and get prices from some of the companies that have advertised. Write down all the calls you need to make, and then make it easy for yourself. Phone the people you know first. (And note that selecting a removal firm is just one part of the very large task of moving.)

- As you break down the project, remember that even five minutes is enough time to get something done. Two phone calls can be completed in that time.

- If there really *is* no time, carve out time from your existing schedule. If you *really* want to write a novel, try getting up half an hour earlier each day (or on weekends). If you really want to do it, you'll find the time.

- You don't always have to start at the beginning. If that first step seems the hardest, start with another part of the project.

- Some people like to do the worst first. If they accomplish what they dislike most, the rest of the project proceeds more smoothly.

● Set small deadlines for yourself: for example, a major desk
organisation schedule might include:
  ★ Purchase desktop organisers by April 20
  ★ Establish a Desk Workbook by April 30
  ★ Finish sorting through papers by May 8.
  For more information, see Chapter 9.

● After each small deadline, promise yourself a small reward.
Perhaps it could be a new paperback or a tennis lesson. After
the entire project is completed, think on a grander scale and
promise yourself dinner out and a film, or tickets to a football
game.

● Try to do things as they occur to you. The more papers you
process as they arrive in the post or the more tasks you
complete as you think of them, the less opportunity you'll
have to procrastinate.

● Ask yourself, 'Is there a simpler way to do it?' Maybe you're
making the task more difficult than it is. Do you really need
to make dessert for the party from scratch or would ice cream
topped with fruit do?

● Ask yourself, 'What's the worst thing that will happen if I *do*
it?' (Perhaps you'll spend a beautiful Saturday afternoon
inside finishing your project, but isn't that better than
spending all Saturday worrying whether you'll feel like
doing it on Sunday?)

● Do nothing! Try sitting with the project in front of you for a
full 15 minutes. People generally become so frustrated by
just sitting there that they dive into the project before the
allotted time has passed!

● Clear your work area of all else so you don't let your eyes
wander.

● If you have one type of project on which you procrastinate,
consider your workspace — perhaps it's simply not
convenient. One client constantly complained that she never
had time to write, though she enjoyed it. When I visited her I
saw why. Her typewriter was stored in its case high in a
cupboard; her notes and files were in another, and her books
were scattered on the floor — she then had to carry
everything to a fourth location where she liked to work.
Simply setting-up was such a big project, small wonder she
never wrote!

- Try tricking yourself: 'If I don't finish writing these letters by 9pm then I won't allow myself to watch my favourite television show.' Working against that sort of deadline can be quite effective!

- Listen to your moods. When you're motivated, use that energy to get the project done. Lots of people laugh at those who use anger as a motivation to scrub the floor or clean a cupboard, but what's so silly about it? It makes them feel better by burning off the excess energy caused by the anger, and they accomplish something they probably wouldn't otherwise.

- Plan an appropriate reason to be motivated. For example, if you have been procrastinating on getting the rugs and windows cleaned, host a Sunday lunch as motivation. Your friends may not care if your house glows, but it will make you feel good if it does.

- Be opportunistic. If your father calls and says he'll be an half hour late dropping by, take that 30-minute block of time and make a stab at something you've put off. Or if a meeting that would have taken a full afternoon is cancelled, consider working on a special project which needs your attention. With a full afternoon, you have a longer period of time to concentrate.

- Consider your 'To Do' list inviolate. Once a task from the project gets written down on that list, then it *shall* be done.

- Tell someone else what your deadline is. Often you will be motivated by not wanting to tell them you didn't meet the deadline.

- Expect problems. You may get sick; the kids may get sick. You may be delayed coming back from your trip. If you anticipate that you really won't have 'all of next week' to work on something, then you may be motivated to start a little earlier.

- If you tend to stall when you're almost finished with a project, maybe you fear being judged once you're finished. Go easy on yourself. At heart, you know it doesn't really need to be perfect.

- If you've promised to get back to someone about a decision but haven't made up your mind yet, call and tell him you haven't made up your mind, but you *will* get back to him.

Then at least you don't add guilt (about not getting back in touch) to your indecision.

● Remember that you really aren't the only one who can do the job well, so delegate to someone else what you don't want to do or hire someone to do it for you. You could also barter with a friend. If she'll organise your files, you can organise her wardrobe.

● Be sure to use your leisure time for leisure. Most procrastinators ruin much of their free time because they are worrying about whether 'tomorrow' is really enough time to get something done. Learning to do things in advance provides the opportunity for worry-free leisure.

● Sometimes procrastination is a decision in itself. If you don't get around to sending for the travel brochures you promised you'd send for, think again. Maybe you really don't want to go away right now.

## *How to help procrastinators*

You can't *make* procrastinators do something they don't intend, but you can encourage them. Here is some advice:

● Discuss the project with them, but make sure you leave them with a sense of control or they'll never do it. Open a discussion about the consequences of a delay. Don't threaten them, but be certain they understand.

● Help them be realistic. Is completing the report for work *and* going to the party a realistic expectation for Wednesday night? Help them realise that they may not be able to do it all.

● Suggest that they break down the project and establish small rewards for finishing certain steps.

● Whatever you do, don't do it for them! Give lots of support and encouragement instead.

● Offer an incentive – a night out, their favourite chocolate cake as dessert, a new record.

It's sometimes said that certain people are so well organised they are even born on their due dates. Well, I had a client whose husband *was* born on his due date, but he certainly wasn't well organised! He put off everything: household chores, fixing things, paperwork, important phone calls. His wife even recalls asking him to fill out some information for her, and it taking him two-and-a-half years to do it. Finally, she figured out how to motivate him. Money was his Achilles' heel, so she promised that if he didn't do certain tasks by certain dates, she was going to hire someone else to do them. The thought of paying someone money pushed him into action. Now all *you* need to do is find the motivator for your procrastinator!

# 2: Managing Interruptions

- You never have the chance to take a nap, but this afternoon you're *so* sleepy and everyone has gone, so you decide to lie down for a few minutes.... The phone rings.

- Finally, you have an hour to work on that project that needs to be finished and you've just got organised when . . . your partner comes home earlier than expected.

- You've just settled down to enjoy a long-awaited cup of tea, and it's the first moment of peace you've had all day.... The doorbell rings, the dog barks, and the baby (who has slept all of 20 minutes) wakes because of the clamour.

Does any of this sound familiar? Probably. Interruptions are very much a part of our lives.

While some interruptions can be prevented, many are inevitable, and the best you can hope for is to manage them. To do so, plan to accomplish the following goals:

- Try to prevent interruptions that can be foreseen.

- Keep interruptions that are inevitable to a minimum.

- Shorten interruptions that occur.

## Planning

Most interruptions come about because the priorities of someone else come into conflict with what you've planned. The electricity board arrives unannounced; your child wants you to get her more juice; your husband thinks you must know where his blue shirt is; the list goes on and on. Here are 18 ways to minimise these types of interruptions:

- Ask friends and family not to drop by without notice. (One friend's mother dropped in unannounced a few days after my friend was married. She and her husband were definitely interrupted, and to make matters worse, her husband jumped up announcing: 'Every man for himself' as they quickly pulled themselves together!)

11

● Group together interruptions that are within your control. If you are taking a day off work so that some furniture can be delivered, for example, use that time as an opportunity to have the plumber come to repair the bath tap and the TV repairperson to check your television's reception. Narrow this block of time as much as possible by scheduling everything for morning or afternoon – if the furniture is to be delivered in the morning, try to arrange for other repair people/deliveries to be in the morning as well.

● If you live in an apartment building with a doorman, ask him to hold packages and deliveries for you. That way you can have items brought up all at one time rather than throughout the day.

● Help your family help themselves. Determine what they most frequently request from you. Food? Help in finding things? Try to arrange things so that they can do it themselves. For example, healthy snack food such as apple slices and juice can be set up in such a way that a four-year-old can get it himself. Even a two-year-old's needs can be met to some extent by making certain she has enough to drink and something to keep her busy (such as a favourite toy which you've hidden away in anticipation of needing some uninterrupted time) while you complete a project. Or if your partner has a particular weakness (e.g. losing things), try to establish a system so that you don't have to be the one who always figures out where things are. (If finding pens is a problem, for example, stock up with so many that he or she can't possibly *not* find one.)

● On a day-to-day basis, anticipate the needs your family may or will encounter and expect you to fulfil. If it's snowing for the first time this winter, even your self-sufficient eight-year-old will need someone to help dig out his boots. Or if your husband likes to flip through the post as soon as he comes home, make certain it's in the same spot as always so he doesn't 'rearrange' the furniture looking for it.

● Teach your family that a closed door or a 'Do Not Disturb' sign means business. One family has a half-serious rule that at certain times the mother is not to be interrupted unless a child is bleeding or the house is on fire. While this is extreme (and the child knows it) it does get the point across.

● Learn to say no. If you feel you've acted as family waitress and kind neighbour one too many times this weekend, and you have no private time of your own, stand your ground. A simple no will sometimes make the interruption go away.

- Set up rewards. If you have half an hour or an hour with no interruptions, promise the children a treat such as playing a favourite game. For your husband, you might prepare a favourite dinner or leave a card for him expressing your thanks.

- The telephone answering machine has been the greatest home invention since sliced bread. Turn it on when you need some quiet time. (See Chapter 3 for additional information about handling such interruptions.)

- As a last resort, leave the house. Sometimes investing in a babysitter − or if children aren't the problem, just simply getting away − is the best way to have uninterrupted time. Go to the library, or a park bench in the summer, and enjoy your time there.

## *Managing interruptions*

- If someone over the age of four is interrupting you, try:
  - ★ 'How can I help you?'
  - ★ 'I'd love to hear about it, but could I come and discuss it once I've finished my project?' (For children, you need to speak of time in relation to something they understand. You might say, 'Can I come and discuss it once you've listened to both sides of your record?')

- Don't prolong a conversation or do anything to extend an interruption. Once you've been interrupted, it's tempting just to stop, but remember that this is the time you intended to devote to something specific (whether it was a nap or paying your bills), so see that you get right back to it.

- Plan for the fact that there *will* be interruptions. If the phone is your main interrupter, there will be times when you don't have your machine turned on, keep small projects near the phone to work on during a conversation. A long cord on a kitchen extension can also permit you to dice food, fix snacks, or prepare lunches while on the phone. Make use of that time.

One woman's husband used to interrupt her telephone calls

with, 'Who are you talking to? What do they want?' After polite requests and frantic hand gesturing requesting that he wait until she was off the phone failed to elicit the proper response, she finally resorted to doing it to *him* when he was on the phone – it worked. So sometimes you may have to use your ingenuity to control certain types of interruptions.

## *Don't be your own interrupter*

- Don't use interruptions as an excuse to avoid your work.
- Don't make the mistake of initiating phone calls or visits to break the peace.
- Don't encourage unnecessary telephone calls from family and friends.
- Don't start another project before you finish the first one. When you have too much going on at once, you interrupt yourself mentally by focusing on the wrong project at the wrong time.
- Don't procrastinate. Once you have the time, use it!

# 3: Telephone Conversations

How many times have you really gained momentum on a job only to be interrupted by a telephone call you really didn't want to take?

How often have you been stuck on the telephone, trying to get off, but were somehow unable to end the converation?

And what about the times you have been put on hold for what seems like an eternity – especially the times when *they've phoned you!*

Or how many times have you phoned someone only to forget one of the reasons you called?

The telephone is a great invention and can be a terrific convenience and time-saver. But few people realise that you don't have to permit it to rule the household by allowing callers to interrupt meals, delay departures, waste your time with needlessly long calls, and otherwise cause inconvenience. Learn to control the telephone so it doesn't control you.

## Establishing a telephone centre

First you need to organise the area around your telephone so that you can efficiently make and receive calls.

- A pad and pencil should be kept by every telephone in the house. Keep an extra pad nearby at all times so that you can re-stock easily. If your pens and pencils tend to 'wander away', buy a pen-on-a-cord and attach it to the telephone.
- Keep your diary, telephone books, dialling code book, and a directory of personal telephone numbers close to the phone used most frequently.

## Before you make a call

Perhaps the easiest telephone habits to alter concern your outgoing calls, and these changes can result in substantial time-saving.

- Establish a 'telephone time', during which you make all necessary calls. By making the calls all at one sitting, rather than throughout the day, you are more likely to keep on with the task at hand rather than digressing and having a chat with someone.
- To avoid having to call a person back again, make notes about what you need to discuss. If you need to make just a few calls, with only a point or two to be discussed with each person, you can easily make such notes in your diary. However, if you're doing lots of phoning (on a regular basis or even just on one day), use your telephone pad for some pre-planning. On the top line of the page you can note the person's name, telephone number, and the date. Beneath that, note the points that need to be discussed. As you talk, you should write down any significant information from the conversation. A typical page might look like this:

JACK'S RENT A CAR

*556 0892      6/387*

---

– What is your daily rate?
– How many free miles?
– Where can the car be picked up and returned?

Record the replies on the bottom and then compare the information with other rent-a-car services you are calling.

- When your calls are completed, transfer important information to your diary (e.g. date you need to follow up with someone) or to your files (questions you asked your accountant regarding your taxes would go in your Tax File). Then throw the sheet away.
- As you dial, concentrate on the call you are making and what you need to discuss. When phoning several people at one sitting there is a tendency to let your mind drift and forget whom you've called.
- Get to the point of your call quickly and stick to it.
- Take care of business before pleasure. If you need to discuss financial matters with your broker, make sure all business is taken care of before discussing the perils of the flu season.
- Don't let a person babble. If their reply begins to wander, don't hesitate to bring them back to the conversation with a

polite but firm: 'Do you have that information or could you suggest someone else for me to call?'

## Ending conversations

Sometimes getting off the phone can be an art in itself. Certain people – you know the type – ignore all the subtle signals you give; they just keep talking. Here are some tips on how to free yourself more quickly:

- Warn them in advance that your time is limited: 'It sounds interesting, but I've got to leave here in five minutes. Can you tell me about it briefly?'

- Try inserting, 'Before we hang up . . .' as a mental warning to the other person that this call will end soon.

- Keep a kitchen timer near each phone, and when you want to get off, set it. When the bell rings, you can announce, 'Well, I have to go. I've got to take something out of the oven.'

- Try pretending someone has arrived at the front door and that you must answer it.

- For the person who calls frequently, you'll soon run out of contrived 'exit' lines. Try being honest with them: 'I really can't spend a lot of time on the telephone. Let's speak briefly when we need to and meet for lunch instead.'

## If you don't know where the time goes . . .

- Conversations last longer than you think. Time them by keeping a clock by the phone. One client limits all calls – not just those that are long-distance – to no longer than five minutes and uses a timer to remind himself.

- If you don't really know why the phone is taking up so much of your time, try logging your calls. Keep a sheet of paper near each phone and list the following: the time of the call, the name of the person with whom you spoke, who originated the call, and the subject and length of the call.

*Time     Person     Who originated     Subject     Length*

A quick scan of the sheet after a week or so will tell you how your telephone time is spent, which will then make it easier for you to determine how to eliminate or shorten certain calls. You may find that you've been taking calls throughout the day when what you really needed was a block of uninterrupted time. Or there may be one person who calls you almost every morning (when you're jammed) just to pass the time. You can solve the problem by suggesting a better time to talk.

## How an answering machine can change your life

The £80 to £200 spent on an answering machine is well worth the investment. Here's why:

- It can receive calls while you're not there, meaning that you get all the information people need to convey to you (appointment cancelled, meeting changed) without your having to be at home.

- As people become more comfortable with speaking to a machine, their messages become longer and more helpful. A machine with unlimited time for recording incoming messages can serve you and many of your callers as a 'secretary'. Lengthy messages can save both parties extra phoning. (A business associate of mine will often phone people *hoping* to get their machine so she can leave one efficient message and be done with it.)

- You can use the machine as a way to screen calls. If you're working on a project or taking a break, you can leave the machine on but monitor who is calling. If it's urgent, you can answer it. If it's not, you can call them back later − at *your* convenience.

- Receiving a call when you're trying to get out the door can be very irritating, because it often means you have to rush for what seems like the rest of the day. A solution? Turn on your machine about 15 minutes before you need to leave. That way you won't be delayed by any calls you don't want or need to answer. If you're on your way to an appointment, be sure to call and confirm before turning on the machine. That will keep you from missing a possible cancellation call.

## Additional ways to control your calls

- Get someone else to answer the phone for you at certain times.

You can return the favour by doing the same for him or her.

• Turn off the phone or unplug it when you don't want to be disturbed, such as at dinnertime.

## *Other telephone tips*

• When you have *lots* of incoming and outgoing calls, keep a list of calls to make and a list of expected returns.

• Avoid 'boxing and coxing' When you leave a message for someone to call you, give a time when you'll be available (and when it will be convenient) to receive the call.

• When leaving messages, provide as much information as possible, being specific and clear, so you can eliminate extra phoning.

• Ask others when it's a good time to call them. If you haven't been able to reach them during your 'telephone time', you'll now have some indication as to when they might be available.

• Return telephone calls. You'll increase your credibility if you do.

• If someone takes messages for you, ask him to repeat back the caller's name and number to ensure he gets the correct information.

• Put long extension cords on your telephone (or consider buying a cordless phone). Then if you need something from your files, you can retrieve it while still talking. It also helps in keeping track of family whereabouts.

One woman came to me because of a problem she and her family were having with the telephone when trying to set up family get-togethers. They said that it usually took 25 phone calls to organise their plans – and that was only among four of them!

The suggestion I offered – and which they now follow – is that they put one person in charge of the plans, and then they do a round-robin to let the others know. That way, each person now gets only *one* phone call with all the information they need as to day, date, time, and place.

The next time you think: 'I can't believe how much time I've wasted on the phone!', remember what you've learned in this chapter and see if there isn't a way to accomplish what you need to do in less time.

# 4: Getting out of the House on Time

One day a friend and I were to attend a meeting together, and about an hour before we were to be there, I had a frantic phone call from her. She'd been running late that morning and had forgotten all her papers for the meeting as well as her diary, which gave the address of where we were to meet. It was too late to go back, so she had phoned me for the address and we had to do without her papers that day.

Another friend constantly forgets things but remembers them before she reaches the lobby of her building. She is always going back up to the flat for her child's lunch, her diary, or the cleaning she wanted to drop off that day. Of course, this often makes her late.

A common reason people run late is because they practise 'at-the-door' planning. They don't consider what they need for the day until they are ready to leave. Or they get everything organised, but leave it in the kitchen or the bedroom where it is all too easily forgotten when they're running out of the front door. Needless to say, this type of leave-taking sets off a poor chain of events all day. Here's how to smooth out your departure.

## Do ahead of time

- Lay out your clothes the night before, this can be done quickly and easily if your cupboards are well organised. Don't hang up anything if it needs to be laundered, mended, and/or ironed. And, if necessary, shoes should be shined before being returned to the cupboard after wearing.
- Set the breakfast table.
- Pack your handbag and/or briefcase and leave them in a convenient spot by the coat cupboard.
- To avoid a last-minute 'key hunt', establish a place where keys are *always* kept.

20

• Think in advance about what you *need* to do in the morning. Add up how many minutes each task will take. To that add on travel time and an additional 15—20 minutes for traffic and 'surprises'. This will allow you to plan exactly how much time you need to get out of the house on time.

• For an especially early morning (or for the person who needs all the help he or she can get in the morning!), leave out — *and all together* — coat, scarf, gloves, hat, handbag, briefcase, keys, money, and anything else you need for a quick exit.

## Set the morning routine

• Make your bed as soon as you get up.

• Use an answering machine to screen morning calls so you don't get bogged down by a conversation that could be held later in the day.

• To avoid congestion in the bathroom, schedule different bath times for family members. Bathing or showering in the evening will reduce friction in the morning.

• Stay with the task you start. Don't hop from room to room as you get ready. As you leave each room, take with you items such as your coffee cup and tidy up as you go.

• Call to confirm your appointment before you leave home and to double check that the person you are seeing is running on time. Never assume that other people are as organised as you are.

• If you're really in a squeeze, ask yourself: 'Okay, what *must* be done now to get me out the door, and what can wait?' (You *must* get dressed; the dishes can wait.) Just keep asking this same question until you're out the door.

## Especially for parents

• Have standing back-up arrangements for what you'll do if your school-age child is sick, if the babysitter or cleaning person is late or doesn't show up at all.

• The night before:

  ★Lay out children's clothing.

★Make lunches.

★Re-pack nappy bag, if appropriate.

• In the morning, get up and be dressed first so you can tend more fully to the children's needs.

• Leave extra time for last-minute occurrences.

## For the chronically late

I'm sure you've heard people jokingly say, 'He's always late — he'd be late to his own wedding!' Well, I've got a sister like that, and she *was* late to her own wedding! She applied her make-up at home but wanted to put on her dress at the place where the wedding was being held, and because she was running so late all her guests saw the bride arrive beautifully made-up — but in blue jeans.

If you're like my sister, here are some tips which might help out:

• Put yourself on a tight and consistent schedule. Routines soon become second nature and make it easier to get moving and get things done.

• Have a clock in every room — even the bathroom.

• Set the clocks a few minutes ahead.

• In your diary, mark your appointments a little earlier than they really are.

• Set a kitchen timer for 15-minute time slots. The bell will remind you how much time has passed.

• Ask a friend to call to get you moving or even stop to pick you up.

# 5. Preserving Personal Time

When I ask people about their personal time, they frequently answer, 'Personal time? You've got to be joking!'

There's no doubt about it. In today's fast-paced society, with so many things to do and so many things to attract our attention, it's very difficult to set aside time for ourselves. Some people spend their personal time taking a relaxing jog in the morning when they can let their minds drift. Other people read a good book. Still others think the best thing in the world is having time to call an old friend.

No matter how you spend such time, you've got to *work* to preserve it. Here are some tips.

## Finding the time

- The first thing you need to do is decide how you can best provide for some personal time. Some people like to schedule it — a workaholic might reserve Sunday afternoons for herself; a mother might schedule a regular babysitter once a week so that she can have time off. One couple I know has standing appointments with a sitter for every Thursday and Saturday night so they know they'll have time off together. Others find it satisfactory to take time as needed; when they are really feeling overwhelmed, then they work to carve out time for themselves.

- Some people steal their personal time from their 'sleeping time' by getting up half an hour or an hour earlier. (Set your alarm earlier by ten-minute increments to adjust gradually to the new wake-up time.)

- You can borrow personal time from 'waiting time' while in your doctor's waiting room as you wait for your appointment, or during a bus or train ride; or you can use the time gained from a cancelled appointment.

- If you have children, make it clear you need time of your own. If you've organised a half-hour activity for them while you have a break, explain to them this is *your* time. Or explain that you'll play or talk with them when their TV show is over or their game is finished.
- To have personal time you must guard your right to it, but sometimes you'll need to be flexible. For example, I take an aerobics class three mornings a week from 7:30 to 8:30 and swim on Saturdays. I wouldn't give up that time for anything. I believe that I've earned it, need it, and that it belongs to me. But of course, in an emergency, I would reschedule my personal time.
- Make a definite decision as to how you want to spend your personal time, or it will simply slip away from you. Do you want to spend it alone? With the family? With friends? And what sort of activity would you like to do?

## How to spend personal time

You no longer have to dream about what you would do with your 'free' time. You can:

- Read.
- Exercise.
- Try a new recipe.
- Clean out a cupboard.
- Organise a photo album.
- Spend more time with your partner or children or catch up with a friend.
- Go to a museum.
- Go to the theatre or cinema.
- Go to a sporting event.
- Take a lesson (ballroom dancing, flower arranging, yoga).
- Buy yourself a gift.
- Write or answer a letter.
- Treat yourself to a manicure, pedicure, facial, haircut, hair colouring, make-up lesson, massage.
- Take yourself out to lunch (enjoy the quiet and being waited on) or for tea and biscuits.

- Be frivolous. Have your astrological chart done; go to a palm reader; go to a psychic.
- Use the time for self-evaluation and assessing what you like about your life and what you want to change.
- Do nothing!
- Learn to play an instrument.
- Practise roller or ice skating, or perhaps anything you've always wanted to do or admired others for doing.
- Take a bubble bath.
- Daydream.
- Browse through an antique shop.
- Start a diary.
- Do a crossword puzzle.
- Paint.
- Listen to music.

After you've done one of the above (or anything else), think about it. Do you feel refreshed and glad you spent the time in that way? Or are you a bit frustrated and afraid you wasted the time? If you don't feel terrific afterwards, try something else. Don't give up your personal time, but find the activity that is right for you. Then make a firm resolve to protect that time, just as you would guard a commitment you made in any other part of your life.

## Beware of time wasters

For each of the following time wasters, there is an obvious solution. In the list below, how often do you recognise yourself?

- Not having a plan; lacking direction.
- Failing to set priorities; trapped by indecision.
- Inability to say no.
- Attempting to take on more tasks than you can possibly handle.
- Failure to delegate; trying to do everything yourself.
- Scheduling activities so that you have too much or too little time for something.

- Putting off something which should be done today.

- Focusing on how busy you are; avoiding priority work.

- Suffering from personal disorganisation; unable to find things because of clutter.

- Jumping from one activity, project, item to the next instead of getting *one* thing done.

- Leaving tasks unfinished and having to re-think what you were doing in order to finish up.

- Getting bogged down by detail instead of keeping your goals in mind.

- Starting a project without having enough information.

- Lacking skills to accomplish what you intend (e.g. having to hunt-and-peck at the typewriter because you don't know how).

- Being kept waiting.

- Being interrupted by the telephone.

- Socialising during times you set aside for projects.

- Being interrupted by visitors who drop in.

- Not getting to the point in a conversation; not saying what you mean.

- Attending meetings without an agenda.

- Not using your commuting or travel time wisely.

- Watching television when you had planned to do something else.

# 6: How to use a Kitchen Timer to Manage Time

A simple kitchen timer can prove invaluable as a reminder system or as an aid in managing small blocks of time. Rather than using the timer on the cooker (which has limited range), buy a portable timer so you can use it in various parts of the house.

## Here are 15 ways to use a kitchen timer

- As a way to time (and limit) your morning shower. Aim for one that is three minutes long.
- As a reminder to make a telephone call.
- As a reminder to try a call again when you got an engaged signal the first time.
- To limit telephone conversations that tend to get lengthy. (Set the timer for five minutes.)
- As an incentive to start something. If you've been procrastinating on a project, set your timer for ten minutes and promise to work that long on what you don't want to do. Chances are you'll no longer feel blocked by the undertaking, but if you do, use the ten-minute system again the next day until you're comfortable with the project or until you're finished with it.
- As a way to get started exercising: 'I'll exercise for just ten minutes.'
- As a way to motivate yourself to do the cleaning: 'I'll spend only ten minutes picking things up.'
- Play 'beat the clock' to get the chores done around the house: 'I'll bet I can clean all the mirrors and glass in less than ten minutes.'
- When working in blocks of time (such as spending half an hour setting up a library for your books). Stop when the bell goes off.

- As a reminder to turn off the oven, the sprinkler, and the like.

- To tell you when it is time for something, e.g. a television special or a favourite radio programme.

- As a way to time a discussion or argument. Each person gets five minutes to present his side of the case.

- To free you from worrying about time. If you come home and have only 45 minutes until you must leave again, set the timer rather than watching the clock. It frees you to focus on something else while guaranteeing that you'll know when it's time to go out again.

- As a way to help a small child cope with waiting. If a youngster wants your attention when you can't give it, set the timer for when you'll be finished with your task. Tell the child to play until the bell goes off and then you'll read her a story.

- As a way to time 'turns'. When two pre-school children get into an unresolvable argument over whose turn it is to play with a certain toy, give each of them five minutes with the item. The ringing bell signals that that turn is over.

# *Section 2*
## *~*
# *Paperwork*

# 7: Books

I've heard of sizeable book collections, but the one belonging to this particular client was ridiculous. Her flat was covered, wall-to-wall, with books. There were books used as end tables, books that supported a missing leg of a bed, and books that lurked in every nook and cranny of the flat. My client had literally to create aisles in the piles of books so that there could be a path through her flat. I got the feeling that part of the local library was housed in her living room.

Regardless of the size of the book collection, most of us have had occasion to refer back to a book we read a few years ago — and then can't locate it. You can't help but wonder: 'Did I throw it out? Did I lend it to someone? Did I store it in a box? Or is it simply lost somewhere on my shelves?'

Here's a way to establish a logical system for your home library so you'll be able to find a book when you need it.

## To establish a system

● Have on hand a few empty cartons for books you may want to donate to charity or store in an attic or basement. Also have a stepladder available to help reach high shelves.

● If you have a modest number of books, gather them together to take an inventory.

● If you have a large library with books in several rooms, tackle this project on a room-by-room basis. Work in blocks of time: Monday in the study, Tuesday in the bedroom, and so forth.

● Divide books into categories. Typical ones for most home libraries include:

★Antiques  ★ Children's books
★Art  ★ Cookbooks
★Baby care  ★ Education
★Biography  ★ Fiction
★Business (usually includes  ★ Gardening
  finance and investing)  ★ Health

★History                      ★ Politics
★Hobbies                    ★ Reference
★Interior decorating     ★ Religion
★Music                       ★ Science
★Mysteries                  ★ Self-help
★Pets                         ★ Sports/fitness
★Photography             ★ Travel

- As you categorise, watch for books which could be donated to a hospital, library, school, or the like. You may even want to try selling some to places that buy old or used books.

- Next, group together books you want to save but that don't need to be accessible (those you're saving for your children, those you don't expect to refer to). You may want to store them in the attic, the basement, or in the upper reaches of a cupboard. Label the boxes clearly!

- Now take an inventory of the books you want to keep and have accessible. Do you have adequate shelf space for them? Perhaps you can build shelves in the kitchen for cookbooks or you may want to buy a free-standing bookshelf for the living room. Whether buying or building, keep in mind that adjustable shelves are helpful because you can alter the heights.

- As much as possible, store your books where you will be using them. Cookbooks should be stored in the kitchen; children's books currently being used should be in the children's rooms; reference books should be near your desk; and so on. Less obvious categories can also be appropriately placed. For example, some people like to put art and biography in the living room, and health and fitness books in the bedroom.

- Select specific shelves where certain books will be stored. Frequently used books should be within easy reach, for example.

- After you have decided where each book category will go, organise the books according to subdivisions. For example, cookbooks might best be subdivided by type of cooking (French cooking, soup cookbooks, and so forth). History books might best be arranged by period.

- Sort alphabetically within each subdivision either by title or author, depending on which you remember first about a book.

- Consider placing some books horizontally, which can provide variation in the look of the bookcase and can make titles easier to read.

- Colour-coding can be a good way to remember visually where a book is. This doesn't mean filing books according to jacket colour! Instead, you build an association between a colour and a certain type of book. For example, in a child's room you might paint each shelf of the bookcase a different colour. Then file animal books on the blue shelf, fairy tales on the purple one, and so forth. Very young children can use this system to help with putting books away if appropriately coloured stickers are affixed to each book.

- If you have so many books that some must be kept out of reach (on high shelves, in cupboards, in double rows, etc.), consider a catalogue system. On index cards, write the book's title, author, and subject, and where it is stored. Buy a file card box and subdivider cards which you can label according to subject category. You can then organise each category alphabetically by title or author.

## Other tips

- If people borrow books from you, create a system so that you'll know where your books are. Use a page in your Desk Workbook (see Chapter 9) to record the book's title, the date it was borrowed, the borrower's name, when he or she plans to return it, and his or her telephone number.

- If you're on the verge of having an unmanageable collection like the client I described earlier, then by all means consider using the public library. She would have been better off if she had made a few trips there herself!

# 8: Diaries

One year in early January I had dinner with a friend who was determined to get organised. She had made a New Year's resolution that '*this* will be the year to reform . . .' As we talked, she started telling me that her new diary system would be the key to her organisation, and she proudly began pulling things from a huge bag she was carrying. Out came a month-at-a-glance diary (so she could see a month at a time), a daily planner for personal appointments, another diary for work only, and a large hardbound notebook for jotting down inspirations. I had to tell her I didn't think this 'system' would ever get her organised − it was just a lot of extra baggage to carry around! As you'll see, she would have been better off had she purchased just one diary. With the right one, she could have kept track of everything.

Diaries come in all sizes and shapes. Some have lovely artwork every few pages; others quote literature; still others are just plain businesslike. Regardless of the kind of diary you use, it must be a convenient one and you should feel comfortable with it. A diary used regularly and effectively can become an important tool in a well-organised life.

- *Use only one diary.* This is the single most important point about diaries, yet some people think they can't live without two or three. The problem with having more than one diary is that you may forget to transfer information from one to another. One business woman kept one appointment diary at home and another at the office − a logical but unwise practice. She switched to a one-diary system the morning she arrived at a restaurant for a meeting only to discover two different clients awaited her − she had set up two breakfast appointments for the same day!

- *Choose the type of diary you feel most comfortable with.* Some people like week-at-a-glance styles, while others prefer to have a page or two devoted to each day. In choosing, keep in mind that a good dairy should be:

33

★Large enough to provide space to record appointments and activities, to make notes (such as questions to ask at your next appointment), and to keep a list of errands and projects to accomplish that day.

★Small enough to carry with you at all times.

A good diary might also include:

★A telephone list (for frequently called numbers)

★An expense record

★Extra pages for notes (handy for jotting down ideas while you're on the go).

- *Write down everything.* Don't trust yourself (or clutter your mind) with having to remember the dinner date with your neighbours next Tuesday. And even if you have a standing Friday afternoon appointment at the manicurist, you can sometimes forget about it if it is not written down.

- When using your diary to record an appointment, write down the address, telephone number, and directions in the space next to the appointment. The more information of this type you write down, the better your diary will serve as a helpful record if you need to go back and verify something.

- Always review your activities at least one week in advance so you'll know what you're to be doing and can make any changes if you're double-booked.

- At the office, leave a photocopy of the day's or week's appointments with your secretary so that he or she always knows your whereabouts.

- Spouses should periodically (daily or every few days) review each other's plans (especially when both carry a day planner) so that each knows when the other will be late coming home or will be going out of town, and also can be aware of and note places where they are to go together.

- Schedules of young children should be noted in the diary of the parent who is responsible for getting them places (or instructing the babysitter to do so).

- When a child becomes old enough to start taking responsibility for his or her own plans, it's time to begin a children's/family calendar — usually best located in the kitchen. Have each family member write on it in their own predetermined colour (choose a colour for family activities as well), so that information about someone or about family activities is easy to spot. Parents should write down plans they make which affect the children, such as 'Sunday dinner at Granny's or, for example, on Tuesday 'Mum late for dinner'. Children should record *all* their plans on the calendar so that if you arrive home one afternoon and find that your child isn't there yet, you can quickly check the calendar to see where he or she is.

- Make a habit of checking the wall calendar *daily* to see if there is information there you need to add to your personal diary. You don't want to schedule a meeting at the time you promised to pick up your daughter and her friends from the ice skating rink.

# 9: Desk Organisation

For many people, their desks are where they live most of the day. And many of these environments are overwhelming disasters. I'm often hired to be a 'desk doctor', and I can't tell you the number of times I've walked in and seen a desk which could easily have been mistaken for the home of a pack rat, yet the client assures me that he or she has 'cleaned up' for my arrival. Referring to the magazine make overs where a woman is transformed into the belle of the ball, one reporter whom I visited noted: 'My desk looks like a "before" and I want it to look like an "after".' She wanted her 'hopeless mess' to become a model of efficiency. With dedication, it can be done, and that's what we'll work towards in this chapter.

I find that most of my clients' problems generally fall into one of three categories:

- *Poor space planning.* They have to keep jumping up and down to get the items they need.
- *Poor work habits.* Each day a few more papers become permanent residents of the 'to do' stack.
- *Indecision.* They have no idea what to do with the stacks of paper on their desks.

Here are some ways to get your desk under control.

## General planning

- Whether you spend one hour or eight at your desk every day, careful thought should go into how you use it. Make it functional!
- For a desk at home, *try to establish a place which is solely for paper-work* (see building suggestions below). Though a storage unit on wheels can make working at the kitchen

36

table bearable, it is not ideal to have to clear your work surface each time the family wants to eat.

- It's preferable to have a desk of your own rather than sharing one.

- Know your work habits. If you like to spread out material as you work, provide yourself with enough space (such as a large desk surface or a long countertop).

- A good chair is as important as a functional desk. Invest in one that is right for you. A chair on wheels is particularly handy.

## Buying a desk

- Shop for a desk with enough surface space so you can spread out your materials.

- Files and supplies should by very accessible. Some desks have this type of storage built into them.

- Sit at the desk in a chair similar to the one you'll be using. The desk should feel comfortable to you, and there should be enough room underneath for your legs.

- I prefer desks which are wider than they are deep. Deep desks lend themselves to pushing stacks of paper into the far corner, making it too easy for things to get lost.

## Building new desk space

- A practical, inexpensive desk can be made by placing a laminated board across two filing cabinets. Such an arrangement will provide a large work surface, with files that are close at hand.

- If you're working with a carpenter, consider a U-shaped counter with storage underneath. It will provide lots of space conveniently within reach.

- One compact way to gain desk space is to build work space in a cupboard. Then just close the door when you're finished for the day!

- If you have a useless cubbyhole in a study, bedroom, living room, or even the kitchen, consider building a desk in that area. You can even add shuttered doors to close off the area when not in use.

- When space is at a premium, build a collapsible counter. But be sure to have shelves or a storage unit nearby for supplies.

## Organising your desk area

- You must be able to find what you're looking for quickly. 'A place for everything and everything in its place' is an important principle to keep in mind.

- To avoid having to jump up and down as you work, plan space nearby for:

  ★Address book
  ★Birthday book
  ★Diary (Though your diary should always be with you when you're out on appointments, it should also have a 'reserved' space on your desk.)

  ★Dictionary
  ★Files
  ★Reference books
  ★Resource Files (see Chapter 13)
  ★Telephone and answering machine
  ★Waste-paper basket

- Materials to have on hand:

  ★Clock
  ★Household Affairs Folder (see Chapter15)
  ★Chequebook
  ★Calculator
  ★Notepads
  ★Stationery
  ★Envelopes
  ★Stamps
  ★Labels

  ★Letter opener
  ★Stapler
  ★Tape
  ★Pens/pencils
  ★Eraser
  ★Scissors
  ★Paperclips
  ★Rubberbands
  ★Ruler

- Organise the above materials according to use. For example, you may use your letter opener more frequently than your stapler, so place it in a more convenient spot.

- A bulletin board is a terrific desk aid, but don't fall prey to putting up notes which stay up until they are yellow. The bulletin board should be used for reminders that *need* to be visible, e.g. dialling codes or postal district maps you use frequently; or 'today' items, such as questions to ask your insurance agent when he returns your call.

# Additional storage

- Any type of work area can benefit from a storage station on wheels with swing-out drawers, storage bins and trays.

- Design and have built a shelving unit to go above your desk to store items such as those just mentioned. The unit should be in the proper proportion to your desk — close to it and low enough to reach without standing up.

- Take advantage of wall space. Stack your files in storage bins that hang from the wall. Ask for 'hanging files' at the stationery store.

- At a stationery store, look for desktop organisers which will store the items you won't be putting in drawers. There are units which can hold a few file folders for current projects; others have space for pens and pencils as well as miniature drawers or cups for items such as rubberbands and paperclips. But don't buy so many that you clutter your desk with unnecessary organisers.

## Establishing better desk work habits

When it comes to desk organisation, stacks of paper are the single biggest problem I see. You don't have time to finish a project, so you leave it until morning . . . You're expecting an answer from XYZ Company by the end of the week, so you'll leave the file out until then . . . You didn't finish reading the mail, so you'll leave it until Monday . . . And the only problem is that by the time 'Monday' comes, it's too late because now there is pile after pile, and it seems it would take weeks to untangle the mess.

Here are some tips to help you become more effective:

- The key is not to let paper and piles keep multiplying. *Process each item as it comes in,* and get it off your desk (see Chapter 12).

- Make it a rule *always to re-file* things. You can establish a special place (such as a desktop standing file) for current projects, but otherwise put everything away.

- Keep your desk free of clutter. It may tempt your eyes to roam, making time at your desk less effective. Put loose papers in clearly labelled files ('To Do', 'To Read', etc.) or colour-coded ones (purple = typist, green = legal matters).

- If you're concerned about remembering where you are going to put some notes you'll need for an upcoming project, note the location on your bulletin board or in the Tickler File (see Chapter 10) under the day or month the project is due.

- If you've had files out of dead storage for a specific project, gather them up when the project is completed and take the time to put them back where they belong.

- Establish a Desk Workbook. Buy a medium-sized looseleaf notebook (you can easily keep the workbook current by simply taking out pages that are no longer relevant), paper, and dividers. It is invaluable for recording ideas in the working/developing stage. Instead of jotting down notes on scraps of paper and never knowing where to find them, you'll have one place to look when you want to refer back to that million-dollar idea you had the other night. Items found in a Desk Workbook might include: a clever paragraph for a sales letter; the punch line for a speech to be written at the end of the week; a new marketing idea; possible titles for a new project; anecdotes; meeting notes. Move this information to a file when appropriate. For example, the punch line for a speech should be moved to a folder labelled 'Speech' once research and writing of the speech is underway. Use the dividers to break the notebook into categories ('Ideas', 'Business Plan', 'Meetings', or whatever you choose).

- Your Desk Workbook (or the bulletin board) is also a perfect place for an assignment sheet that will keep track of ongoing projects. List the date the assignment was given to you (or when you assigned it to someone else), a description, a progress report, comments, and the due date.

- To keep track of deadlines, use your Tickler Files or your diary. Be sure to note a project's deadline on a date earlier than when it is due so you will be sure to finish it on time.

- Set aside time daily for doing paperwork. Choose an hour when there are few distractions — if at home, in the early morning before the family gets up, or if at work, before the staff comes in. During this time, use an answering machine to screen calls or have your secretary hold calls, or have a co-worker answer your phone (you can return the favour at another time).

- Use your desk clock as an important ally. If you're procrastinating on something, tell yourself you'll work on it for 'just 15 minutes'. And use the clock to help you stop early enough so you will have time to put things away at the end of the day.

- Clean up your desk every night so there's no chaos when you begin the next morning.

## What to do when your desk is a disaster

Many of my clients are truly frantic because their desks are such a mess. They can't find slips of paper on which they wrote important phone numbers; they know they received information they sent for, but now it's buried in a pile of paper; they were working on a chapter of a novel, but now the notes for the next chapter are gone . . .

Here's how I counsel them when I make a 'house call':

- Address your desk problems in blocks of time. You may be able to straighten out the clutter in a few hours or you may need a weekend. Sometimes it's better to devote a couple of hours a day to the job until you're done.

- Have on hand a waste-paper basket, a pen, file folders, labels and any other desk organisational aids I have discussed above which suit your needs.

- Clear the space you want to organise (the desk surface, one of the drawers, etc.). Then make a big pile of all the paper.

- Evaluate each item, categorise it, and put it away (in the desk drawer, in a file, in one of the desk organisers, etc.), *throwing out* as much as possible (see Chapter 10).

- Even when you're feeling overwhelmed, just keep sorting and categorising. If you devote the necessary time, your desk *can* be cleared.

- Re-read this chapter's 'Establishing better desk work habits' periodically. The tips offer the key to keeping your desk clear once you're there.

# 10: Filing Systems

Most people have trouble with filing. I once had a client who was truly desperate because of an overflow of paper. She finally took to carrying all her important papers in a tote bag everywhere she went. 'I didn't want to put them down at home, because I was afraid I wouldn't be able to find them again,' she said.

So much material bombards us in this information-filled world, that it is often overwhelming to sort through it all and store it for future reference. The solution is a personal filing system that will store all pertinent information you and your family need. I can help you create that system — I've done it for the desperate as well as the not-so-desperate.

So whether you've turned to this chapter because you're drowning in piles of paper or whether you have a fairly organised system which you just don't keep up, there is hope. It will take perseverance and some time, but there is a way to create a filing system where it will take you no more than five minutes to locate a piece of paper, no matter how long it's been since you saw it last.

## Common filing mistakes

There are three common mistakes people make when filing:

- They create the 'Now where would I have filed that?' syndrome. By not establishing a logical system, they have trouble remembering how to find what they've filed.
- They establish a workable system — but don't keep up with it. If you have more than 10 or 12 pieces of paper waiting to be filed, you've fallen into the 'I'll do it tomorrow' trap.
- People file 'in perpetuity'. Just because you thought a certain piece of paper might come in handy in 1980, there may be no good reason to still have it on hand in 1988.

## *Establishing a system*

The most effective filing system is one that is:

● Simple

● Easy to understand

● Easily accessible to the family members who will use it.

You don't want a system that is so complicated you or your family will need written instructions to figure it out.

● First, you're going to need to set aside time to re-organise your system. If you have a limited number of items to be filed, it may take half a day. If you have extensive home files, plan to spend three days or so (or an hour a day for two or three weeks). In the end, it will save you time and make accessible all the information that is important in your life.

● Next, invest in a good, sturdy filing cabinet. Whether it is a one- or a four-drawer unit depends on your filing needs. Allow room to grow!

● Plan that your files will ultimately be stored near your work station.

## *Alphabetical or colour-coded?*

There are two simple systems for establishing a filing system, and you need to choose one before you begin. Both are quite workable, so pick the one which best suits your personality.

● *Alphabetical.* The word-oriented individual is probably best suited to the traditional alphabetical system of filing. The key element here is choosing appropriate titles so that the folder will be where you expect it to be. For example, if you're starting a file for ideas for a new career, should you call the new file 'New Job', 'Career Ideas', 'New Career', (or 'Career, New')? This will obviously make a difference in how the folder gets filed. How to decide? *Title it as you most often think of it.* Monitor yourself for a few days and see how you refer to the subject. If you say to a friend, 'I'm thinking of looking for a *new job,'* then 'New Job' would likely be the best title for the file.

● *Colour-coding.* The more design-oriented person might select colour-coding. Here's how to do it:

★Decide on a colour system that will work best for you; for example, pick a different colour for each member of your family — Dad is blue, John is red, Jane is green, and so on. These colours should be consistent throughout the home; John's toothbrush, towels, etc. — as well as his file folders — should be red.) Or, you can use this system for different subjects: insurance is green, travel information is blue, and so forth. Colour-coding speeds filing and acts as insurance against misfiling. Your memory responds to colour first, so when you want the insurance folder, you automatically think 'green'.

★Apply this colour scheme to the files themselves by using coloured folders and file labels or tabs so you can easily pick out the proper colour and category.

★Make a colour key that will explain the system to everyone who wishes to use the file, and have the key within easy access.

● Some people do a combination of alphabetical and colour-coding. The coloured folders are filed alphabetically. It makes retrieval within the file drawer easier. In my filing system, any client-related information is stored in blue folders, and each folder is filed alphabetically by the client's last name.

## Step one: getting started

● Have on hand:
  ★Pen or marker
  ★File folders
  ★File labels which match the colour of your file folders
● Choose a work area with plenty of space.
● Gather together all the miscellaneous papers you want to file as well as any existing files you may have.
● Evaluate the type of information you want to keep to begin developing file categories. Of course, the categories will vary according to your interest, but they will probably include some or many that are listed below. Following each category, I have included some of the items which might be filed there. (As discussed previously, the exact title you choose for each file is the one which will work best for you.)

★*Bargains* — listings of the best places to shop for certain items, articles about discounted items.

★*Car* — log book, owner's manual, mileage chart.

★*Cash receipts* — receipts for major purchases such as appliances, jewellery, television, furniture, home maintenance equipment, as well as your 'New Purchases 198 __ ' list for the year (see Chapter 19 for details).

★*Consumer information* — articles on topics such as how to complain, listings of whom to contact for various problems.

★*Contracts* — agreements between you and people who work for you or for whom you work.

★*Correspondence* — letters you want to keep for reference (each family member should have a separate file).

★*Credit records* — list of credit card account numbers with name, address, and phone number to contact in case the card is stolen; instalment contracts.

★*Employment* — past and present resume; certificates of pay, employee benefit information, pension records from previous employers.

★*Financial planning* — budget related items, financial goals, financial planning articles.

★*Gift lists* — lists of gifts given in previous years as well as an on-going list for the current year.

★*Guarantees and warranties* — warranties, instruction manuals, lists of authorised service centres.

★*Hobbies* — articles or information about a hobby you pursue.

★*Housing, owned* — home improvement receipts, records of land transfer taxes, list of purchase price, closing and selling costs.

★*Housing, rented* — copy of the lease rental agreement, pictures showing move-in condition of rental property.

★*Important documents* — photocopies of documents such as birth certificates, passports, marriage licence, divorce papers, deeds; originals should be kept in a safe-deposit box (see Chapter 20). Photocopies of family wills (originals are sometimes kept by your solicitor. In addition, your social security number, driving licence; and information regarding the whereabouts of important documents and names and addresses of personal advisers — all of which are contained on your Financial Master Lists (see Chapter 17).

★*Insurance* – copies of all policies. List of policy numbers, names of insured persons and possessions, issuing company, agent, type and amount of coverage. Personal Property Inventory (see Chapter 19) including original purchase price of valuable items and photos showing especially valuable or unusual possessions (keep another copy of the Inventory in your strongbox and one in your safe-deposit box).

★*Interior design* – names of recommended designers, articles about home design, photos of other homes you like.

★*Investments* – records of stock or bond purchases and selling prices; transaction slips (broker's purchase and sales statements); brokerage statements.

★*Medical history records* – history of family illnesses (see Chapter 11). Each family member should have a separate, colour-coded file.

★*Reviews, restaurants and cinema* – articles giving recommendations.

★ *Trust information* – Trust correspondence and copies of documents (original documents should be stored in safe-deposit box).

★ *Voluntary work* – material and correspondence pertaining to any voluntary organisation with which you work.

● Consider establishing a special category in your own name with items such as reviews of books you'd like to read, shops you want to visit, craft ideas you might pursue. Such a file can help absorb lots of miscellaneous items that don't merit a file of their own but is information you would like to keep.

## Step two: the process

● Overwhelming as it may seem, go through the stack of papers you've collected piece by piece, making a decision about where to file each paper – try to handle each paper only once!

● As you evaluate each piece, ask '*How do I plan to use this information?*', not 'Where should I put this?' For example, a business card of someone you met from Cardiff might be filed in 'Travel' rather than with other business cards because you hope to visit him the next time you are there.

- If you're stuck, put that piece of paper aside and review it again when you've finished processing the others. Where it belongs may be clearer later.

- Keep working through your papers until you're completely finished. It may take several hours or days, but it will be worth it! You'll have an organised system that will work well for you.

## Step three: develop good filing habits

- Depending on the file, there are different ways of organising within it. For example, the information in a file of correspondence with one company (perhaps concerning a complaint) might best be filed *chronologically*, with the most recent letter on top. The information in a file of correspondence with many companies would best be filed *alphabetically* by company. Choose the system that makes sense for each of your files.

- Staple, rather than clip, relevant material together. Paperclips tend to catch on other papers.

- Store ongoing activities and projects in their own file folder, clearly labelled so you don't have to go through the file to see what's in it. Sometimes people make the mistake of assuming they can stack something on their desk since they'll be finished with it 'soon'. You'll be much happier if there's 'a place for everything, and everything in its place'.

- Divide larger projects into several folders to facilitate retrieval. For example, your voluntary efforts for a conference might be broken down into 'Conference Publicity', 'Conference Brochure,' 'Conference Mailing Lists'.

- If you've had a difficult time deciding where to file a certain piece of paper, consider cross-referencing between two (or more) files. Put a reference slip in each file where the paper *could* have been filed, giving the exact location of the item. This is more efficient (and less bulky) than making multiple copies of something which might fit into one of several categories.

- If you must have the complete copy in another file (for example, something you want on file at home and at the office), make a photocopy of it instead of trying to copy the important points by hand.

- If you must remove papers from a file for any period of time, leave a note as to where they are.
- And always remember to keep frequently used files in an accessible spot.

## Step four: how to maintain your filing system

- File regularly. Choose a basket or create a 'To File' folder. Establish a set time to file — at least twice a week, and preferably daily.
- Keep files lean and current by taking out information you haven't worked on in six months or more. Establish 'Inactive' project files (appropriately titled) and store them in an accessible spot (bottom drawer of filing cabinet? cardboard file box in cupboard?), but be sure not to mix them in with your active files.
- The easiest way to maintain a file is to sift through it every time you use it and throw out material you no longer need. This way you can easily maintain your files, providing for an orderly, up-to-date system with little or no effort.
- If there are files you do not use regularly, choose a time once every three months or so to look through them and weed out the items you no longer need. With entire files you won't be needing soon, place them in 'inactive' storage.

## Establishing tickler files

Tickler Files for items you want to be reminded of are invaluable to being organised. The files are designed to 'tickle' your memory and keep track of details you don't want to think about or have on your desk until needed.

- You will need 18 file folders. Of these, 12 should be labelled for each month of the year, five should be reserved for each day of the business week (Monday to Friday), and the sixth and final folder should be labelled 'Weekend'.
- The monthly Tickler Files will remind you of long-term

items. You can date file your optician's business card in order to remind you to make an appointment to see him in January. Or perhaps you've been told to follow up on something in six weeks — these reminders should all be placed in the appropriate monthly Tickler File. You may want to keep an index card reminding you of upcoming birthdays on file here (see Chapter 38). I also note down on a card when I should expect an insurance renewal, and I file it in the appropiate month. Other items to be date-filed here might include a pet's vaccination schedule, a note about family check-ups in September, a reminder to get heavy coats out of storage in October, and the like.

- The daily Tickler Files will help you organise the papers you need for projects to be done on a certain day. A postcard you receive on Saturday notifying you of a dental appointment you will have to change should be put in Monday's file to remind you to call and schedule a new appointment. An article you want to send to your mother might be filed under Wednesday — the day you plan to write her. A note about a question for your insurance agent whom you need to call on Thursday should go in that day's file. A marketing questionnaire you plan to fill out while waiting for your son to take his piano lesson on Tuesday should be filed appropriately. Weekend files might hold such items as film negatives to be developed, photos to be framed, or a note about the kind of seeds you want to look for at the garden centre. As you take care of each item on the appropriate day, discard the reminder. If for some reason you are unable to process something, select another day in which to file it and take care of it on that day. (Make it a top priority, if you've had to delay it once.)

## *Don't bother to file*

- All the business cards you receive. While you'll want to put valuable contacts in your address book, many people who give you their card you'll never see again. Bind such cards together with a rubber band and store the bundle in your Resource Files (see Chapter 13). If eventually you do want to contact someone, you can retrieve the appropriate card and create a 'Contact' card for them. Otherwise, you can look through the collection periodically and toss out the ones you don't expect to need any longer.

- Papers or clippings you don't really need. If you're wavering on whether or not to file it, follow your impulse to throw it out. Chances are it really *won't* come in handy.
- Catalogues or bulletins that (being realistic) you know you won't refer to.
- Duplicates of anything.
- Information that is obsolete, such as house prices of three years ago.
- Junk mail.
- Chain letters.
- Fliers people insist you take.
- Old notes.

# 11: Health Records

Everyone should keep a complete record of their health. (And of course, parents must assume responsibility for their children's health records.) The history of the diseases you've had is important to any medical professional who serves you. In addition, you need to keep records about your reactions to various medicines. If a new doctor needs to prescribe an antibiotic for you, he or she will need to know which ones (if any) have caused negative reactions in you.

## To establish a system

- For filing purposes, each family member should have his or her own colour.
- Buy index cards in the appropriate colours or use white cards with appropriately coloured file labels to denote each family member's colour.
- On each person's card, record the following information about significant illnesses or doctor's visits:

| MEDICAL RECORD | | JOHN JONES | |
|---|---|---|---|
| Date/Doctor | Reason for visit | Medication (and instruction) or Immunisation | Reaction |
| | | | |

- For adult family members, keep an accurate record of illnesses or health problems severe enough to merit a visit to the doctor. For your own information, note frequent colds or headaches and your reactions to various types of over-the-counter drugs. If you need to see a doctor for persistent headaches, you'll have accurate information, or if you want to know which cold remedy doesn't make you sleepy, you can check your notations.

- For children, note immunisations and major illnesses such as chicken-pox so that later in life your children will have a medical history to which they can refer. While you may not want to keep track of each time your child goes for a check-up, it will be helpful to note the date of an ear infection and what medication was used. That way if the illness recurs you'll know what medicine your child was given and how effective it was. If you have more than one child, a written record of this information is vital! There's no guarantee that you'll remember who reacted badly to a certain antibiotic or who had chicken-pox five summers ago.

- Store these cards in your Health Records file in your filing cabinet.

# 12: Post

Post quiz

- Are there stacks of magazines and newspapers in every room of your home?
- Has personal correspondence been lying around for so long that it's begun to collect dust?
- Do you sometimes RSVP to an event very late or not at all?
- Do you forget to make note of upcoming meetings or social engagements?
- Do you occasionally get bills stamped 'Final Reminder— Payment Overdue' and realise you must have misplaced the first two bills?
- Do you have a pile of junk mail you're saving 'until I have time . . .'?
- Have you ever found uncashed cheques lying around?
- Do you have to throw things out?

If you answered 'yes' to one or more of these questions, read on.

Many people have a love/hate relationship with the post — they love to get it, but hate to deal with it. One man I know wanders through the house dropping the post wherever he finishes reading it — on the TV, in the kitchen, or in a bureau drawer — anywhere but where it belongs. He says he 'likes to let his mail age a little bit' before he does anything with it.

I've nicknamed the daily arrival of the post 'information blues time'. It's the major reason so many people feel as though they are drowning in paper. What's more, there's no stopping it. Through rain, sleet, snow and hail that postman is going to continue to contribute to your growing pile of unread post.

Lots of people like to let their fingers do the walking to pick out the 'good stuff' first, but the problem is that they never find time to sort through the remainder. For that reason, when it comes to mail management, *rule number one is you must deal with the post daily*. Fifteen minutes each day is painless compared to what you may face if you let it pile up.

*Rule number two is don't shuffle the post.* Make a decision about each item as you handle it and then follow through.

In addition, here's what you need to do to successfully fight the daily deluge:

## To start

- Choose a specific time and place to process your post, and have a large waste-paper basket handy.
- First, sort the post according to family member. Your stacks will be more readily manageable if you go through the magazines and catalogues first and then add letters to the top of each pile.
- Establish a set spot for leaving each person's post so he or she will know where to look for it each day.
- If a family member is out of town, store his or her post in a manilla envelope so there will be no chance of misplacing anything.
- Next, sort your own post using the following categories:
  ★To Throw Out
  ★To Ask Someone About
  ★To File
  ★To Call
  ★To Do
  ★To Read.
  Here are coping strategies for items in each category:

## To throw out

- Instead of asking yourself, 'Could I possibly use this one day?', ask 'What's the worst thing that could happen if I throw this out?' If the answer is 'nothing', then toss it out.

## To ask someone about

- Place items which require the comments of another person with the rest of that family member's post.

- Attach a post-it note (a glue-backed piece of notepaper, which adheres to the item but comes off without leaving a mark and is available at stationery stores), and write down your thoughts about the item (e.g., 'This looks fun. Will you go with me?' or 'Is the March 26th store charge yours? If not, there's a billing error.') so that you won't have to re-read it later.

- Staple all pertinent information from the envelope together (travel brochure, agent's business card, price list, etc.) so nothing will get lost.

## *To file*

- Papers that do not require immediate action (insurance policies, tax forms you receive in advance, some legal documents) can be filed.

- Bills should be filed in your Household Affairs Folder under 'Unpaid Bills' (see Chapter 15) so they can be paid all at once or just prior to their due date.

- Establish Tickler Files (see Chapter 10) for those items which can't (or needn't) be resolved immediately. If you're thinking of registering for a class that starts in a month, put the course information in the folder for the appropriate month so that you can consider it as the registration date gets closer. If you've received a flier about a free event that you'd like to attend on Wendesday night, put the notice in Wednesday's folder.

## *To call*

- Can a matter be handled more quickly by phone than by letter? For example, ordering from a catalogue can probably be done more quickly by phone.

- If the place you need to contact is closed for the day, put the item on your list of things to do for the next day.

- Remember to group the calls you make. It wastes time to scatter them throughout the day.

## *To do*

- The items on your list of things to do are the ones which require *action*, and several steps may be involved. Start with the most important items first. For example, notice of a returned cheque or an invitation requiring a written RSVP should be acted upon as soon as possible, while renewing a magazine subscription or answering your aunt's monthly letter can wait a little.

## *To read*

- Be selective. Read only what is important or what interests you.
- Thumb through incoming publications and tear out information of special interest. Toss out the journal or magazine, and keep the articles in a file marked 'On-the-Go Reading'. Every day select several articles to carry with you. When you find yourself waiting in a queue or at the dentist's office, pull out your reading. When finished, throw the item out or mark where it should be filed.
- Donate back issues of magazines before the stacks build up. Hospitals, libraries, schools, and homes for the aged will be very appreciative.

## *Sample 'mail call' and solutions*

Below are some other typical items which come in the post and advice on how to handle each one.

- *A reminder of a 6-month dental check-up.* Make certain the appointment is marked in your diary. Confirm the office address and phone number, and note them down in your diary next to the appointment. Throw out the notice.
- *A programme for the upcoming concert season — but you're not sure you want to attend.* Even though you're still debating whether or not to go, note in your diary (in pencil) any of the dates which interest you. Otherwise, you may book something else for those times. Then put the programme in your

Tickler File where you can review it again at a later date. If you need to order tickets by the end of the week, file the programme in your Friday Tickler File. Otherwise, file the programme in an appropriate monthly Tickler File. Just be sure to file it where you'll be sure to see it before your order needs to be in. (If orders must be in by October 1, for example, file the programme in the September folder.)

- *Business correspondence which requires a reply.* As you read the letter, circle specific questions as a reminder to answer them. Then jot down key points on the letter itself for you or your secretary to draft a response. Put in on your 'To Do' list for the next day.

  If you have lots of standard business correspondence, you may find that making a correspondence book will save time. Take paragraphs from the best of your recent correspondence, organise them by subject, and number them. Then you need note only the paragraph numbers you want and your secretary can use her copy of the book to write the letters. It's a fast way of producing accurate, well-written replies!

- *Personal correspondence.*

  ★Phone a reply.
  ★Carry notepaper or postcards with you, and write a note when you have a spare moment or while waiting for an appointment.
  ★Record a taped reply.
  ★Write one letter and make copies. Some people do a family 'up-date' letter during the holiday season. One woman who was inundated with kind words from many people during a long illness found this was the only way to keep up with her correspondence.

- *Change of address note from someone you know.* Enter the information in your address book right away and throw out the card.

- *Notice informing you of a coming meeting you need to attend.* Write down the date in your calendar and throw the letter out. Keep the agenda, if there is one, in the appropriate Tickler File.

- *A piece of mail that gives you a good idea for a new project.* If you're inspired, start on it now. Otherwise, file it in your

Tickler File under the day or month when you expect to have time to develop the idea.

- *Catalogue from a company you like*. Thumb through it and mark the pages with items of interest. Contact the company by post or phone. If you prefer to give your potential purchase a little more thought, put the catalogue in your Tickler File under the day or month when you might be better prepared to decide (e.g. after paying your bills).

- *New catalogue from an unknown company*. Scan the first few pages. If the information doesn't catch your interest immediately, toss the catalogue out.

- *Business magazine*. Use the 'rip and read' method. Scan the contents (or the magazine) for articles of interest. Tear them out and file them in your 'On-the-Go Reading' file (described above).

- *Other magazines* (fashion, sports, architectural design). Save these for when you have some spare time. Put them with your leisure reading (on the bedside table? by the couch in the sitting room? – wherever you usually read for pleasure.) The material will be waiting for you when you really *do* have time!

# 13: Resource File

Can you identify with any of the following comments?

'I remember that tailor I used a few years ago — he'd be perfect to repair my suede jacket, but I can't remember his name . . .'

Or: 'I'd really like to get back in touch with that man I met at last year's conference to talk to him about a career change, but I have no idea how to contact him . . .'

Or: 'Who was it that Mum used to repair her china? She probably doesn't even remember . . .'

Or: 'The Jones family has moved, but who was that doctor they said was such a good allergist?'

A resource file can solve all these problems and more by providing you with a total system for keeping track of people whom you might like to contact again. Unlike names in a personal telephone directory, these people aren't necessarily individuals you contact regularly — just people you might need one day. Here's how to keep track of them.

## Establishing a resource file

● You'll need:

  ★Index cards in different colours (green for personal contacts, red for home resources, blue for medical, etc.).
  ★Index card dividers
  ★Container for holding index cards.

I like using a card catalogue system because each index card provides plenty of room for writing complete information about the person and/or the service. The system is also easy to update, because you simply add another card if you find someone new, or throw out a card if someone moves or a service goes out of business. In addition, there's always room on the card for adding new details.

## *Contact resource cards*

- Part of your resource file should consist of cards you make with the names of your personal contacts − people whom you've met at parties or conferences or to whom you've been referred by friends. Whenever you need advice, help, or special treatment, you can check the cards to see who might be of help. Update your cards with additional information you get about the person. Add new cards when you make new contacts.

- A typical contact resource card might look like this:

```
Mary Jones                    Met at ASPW Conference      11/87
629 North Avenue
Kingsbourne
Hertfordshire
451 0391

Special knowledge of personnel job market; worked at XYZ for 12 years

Consultation fee: £30/hour

Husband: Mark
Children: Sam and Alex

20/12/87 phone conversation: discussed training I would need to work in
personnel field
```

- List why this person is of interest to you; include special knowledge and skills.

- Be sure to write down how you met the person or who referred you to him or her. Also note the date of the first meeting or recommendation.

- List fees.

- Record the names of spouse and/or children in order to facilitate personal conversations.

- If the person might be someone you will get to know better, you may want to find out his or her date of birth and make a note of it here.

- List dates and notes about conversations and meetings.

• As you prepare to put your cards into the index card container, you will need two of your card dividers. Label one 'Contacts' and the other 'Home Services' (information to follow). Some people file all of their cards alphabetically by name within each of these two groupings. Other people find that they forget names, so filing by category makes the information more readily accessible. For example, suppose you have some work to be done which will soon require the services of a photographer. You meet one you like but know that you'll never be able to remember his name two months from now. Label an index card divider 'Photographers' and use it to file the card on this fellow and on any other photographers you hear about or meet. If you decide to file by subject rather than by name, be consistent. (An index card divider labelled 'Contacts – General' can be a catch-all for those for whom it isn't worth creating a category.)

## *Home service resource cards*

• On each card, list the company (or person), the address, the telephone number, exactly what you used their services for (if you have), the date, and what you paid for the service.

• A sample card might look like this:

---

REPAIRS—CHINA AND GLASS

AAA Company             Recommendation by: Mother     3/22/85
5 Great Oak St.,
London W19.

286 6130

Repairs glass and china; antique porcelain and ceramics are specialities; work takes minimum of two weeks

Repaired chipped goblet, 5/85, £15

---

- If a resource has come through a referral, note from whom you received the referral and the date.

- As you note details, be very specific. For example, one cobbler may be great at altering the height of heels; or one cleaner may be good at knitwear while another is better at cleaning coats.

- Additional resources can be gained by reading the 'service' articles featured in many magazines. You can note information about the ones which might be of use to you and add them to your file.

- Use card dividers to create appropriate categories for your needs. Typical categories of home resources might include the following.
   ★ Babysitters or Child Care Services ★ Books (remainder shops or places to donate books) ★ Cabinetmaking ★ Carpentry ★ Charities (for clothing or furniture donations) ★ Cleaners (some may have specialities) ★ Cleaning Equipment ★ Cleaning Services ★ Clothing, Children's Resale ★ Designers, Interior ★ Desk Supplies ★ Dressmaker ★ Kitchen supplies ★ Repairers ★ Art ★ Antiques ★ Appliances ★ Appliances, small ★ Books ★ Chandeliers ★ China ★ Clocks ★ Dolls ★ Fireplaces ★ Frames ★ Furniture ★ Glass ★ Hats ★ Lace ★ Leather ★ Marble★ Needlepoint ★ Paintings ★ Photographs ★ Quilts ★Reupholsterers ★ Rugs ★ Umbrellas ★Toys, resale ★ Window Cleaning

Once you've set up a Home Service resource file, you'll soon find it invaluable. Being able to locate rapidly all the home services you need will save you hours of telephoning and searching for the right person to mend your iron or the right shop to go to for a certain type of cleaning liquid.

But when it comes to the 'Contact' resource cards, you may one day astound your friends as a client of mine has done. Acquaintances would call him, and he would immediately place who they were and launch into a very friendly conversation: 'How's Sue? What about the boys? Are they still enjoying football?' and so on. He was never at a loss as to who had called him. His secret? His resource file was always close at hand, and as soon as he heard the name of who was calling, his fingers were searching for the right card to tell him *exactly* who it was!

# Section 3
## ~
# Financial Records

# 14: Banking

From an organisational standpoint, there are two major difficulties when it comes to banking. The first concerns the chaos which can ensue if your chequebook and records are not kept up to date. But an accurate, well-maintained chequebook can reduce your risk of a bank error going unnoticed, and it can save you a lot of aggravation at tax time.

The second type of difficulty involves the time which can be wasted while trying to get your banking done. How often have you fumed because the queue at the bank was so long? I have some tips to help you with that, too.

## Establishing a system

- When it comes to efficient record-keeping, one of the most important decisions to make is your choice of chequebook. I recommend using the larger desk-style chequebooks for the simple reason that it provides more room for explaining each cheque or deposit.

- Clients frequently protest: 'But what about the cheques I need to write when I'm away from home?' The solution is simple. When you order your desk-style chequebook, also order a small number of cheques in the portable chequebook format. The small chequebook should be used when you are on the go. Because you have an entire chequebook with you, you are automatically reminded to record the cheque. *Then make it a habit to note the date, cheque number, to whom it was written, and the amount in your main (desk-style) chequebook when you do your daily paperwork that evening.* I find that people who carry a single cheque with them forget to record it when they get home because the lone cheque provides no system to remind them. One man I know takes a cheque with him in the morning and then forgets to write down the amount for which he wrote the cheque. His wife says he regularly wastes time bemoaning the fact that he can't remember how much the cheque was for. The auxiliary chequebook will solve all that.

- Be sure to note *every* cheque you write in your main chequebook. (You must be equally diligent with your auxiliary chequebook, but there you need record only those cheques you write while you're away from home.) Record the number of the cheque, the date, to whom it was written, and the reason for the expenditure. (This will help substantiate tax deductions as well as clarify budget expenses.)
- Deposits should also be carefully noted, and on each deposit slip, be sure to note what the source of the income is for tax purposes.
- Balance your main chequebook after each entry so that you have an accurate view of your bank balance. (You need not balance your auxiliary chequebook since it reflects only a portion of the cheques you write.)
- Keep all your deposit slips and cheque stubs together in a folder until you need them to balance your chequebook. When your statement arrives, you will compare your slips against the bank's record, and once each deposit is verified, you can then put the slips with the appropriate bank statements.
- When your statement comes, balance your account right away. The longer you wait, the more complex it will become because additional cheques and deposits will have to be accounted for.
- Make checkmarks next to cheques and deposits that are verified and make a circle by those that have not yet appeared on the statement.
- At the end of the year, the Deposit slips and cheque stubs Folder should be stored with your Household Affairs Folder (see below) where they will be easily accessible yet out of the way.
- It is generally recommended that you keep such files for at least six years — business-related records may need to be kept longer.

## *Personal banking*

Nothing is more irritating than waiting in a long queue in order to withdraw *your* money.
- If you are shopping for a new bank, you'll naturally be considering what services are offered and what interest rates are charged. But in addition, consider how efficiently your

transactions will be handled: Are there usually long queues? How quickly can you see an assistant manager if you have a problem? Does the bank have quick deposit or automated cash dispensers? Whether or not the bank will make life easier for you is almost as important as the services performed and the rates charged.

- If you need to do banking in person, visit the bank during periods of least activity, which vary according to the bank and the neighbourhood. Generally, it's best to avoid lunch hours (11:30am−2:00pm) as well as paydays, which generally fall on Thursdays and Fridays. Monday mornings can be busy as people come in to take care of financial matters after the weekend.

- Have your deposit and withdrawal slips already made out − and handy − before you go to the bank. You will save time and perhaps be more accurate since you've made them out in the privacy and quiet of your home or office.

- Depositing by post is another alternative. However, you run the risk of the envelope being lost. In addition, you lose any interest you might have earned with an interest-bearing account during the two or three days that the cheque is in the post.

- Automated cash dispensers are usually faster than waiting in the bank queue. The pluses are convenient hours and less waiting time; the minuses are mechanical breakdowns such as not being able to get money when you had expected to or having to wait because the machine has 'eaten' your card.

- Banks are beginning to charge for more and more services. If you are overdrawn and therefore paying for withdrawals try to plan ahead to minimise the number of times you need to do so. This will also save time. (If you're budgeting accurately, you should know exactly how much to withdraw for the week.)

I have a friend, Laura, who is as casual as I am precise, and when I think of organised banking, I *don't* think of her. Right after her wedding reception, Laura ran to her bank's nearest automated cash dispenser − in her wedding dress, mind you − to deposit wedding gift cheques before leaving for her honeymoon. After counting up the cheques and filling out several slips, she deposited her cheques. Later, fear clutched at her when she realised that if the machine made a mistake, they would have lost their 'nest egg'. The next morning she phoned a bank representative who assured her that if she deposited it, everything would be all right. Well, Laura spent the next two weeks of her honeymoon frantically worrying about her deposit. When they got home, they found their account credited for *more* money than she had listed. She had forgotten to enter a cheque, and the bank corrected her error! Her finances may have ended up in order, but what a chaotic way to start off a marriage!

# 15: Bill-Paying

Perhaps you can identify with my friend who remarked how much he enjoys a good meal or a fun night out, 'But it's so depressing when it's time to pay the bills ...'

As you know, the only thing worse than paying a bill is discovering that you *didn't* pay it and are now being billed for a finance charge. Time and again, I visit clients who have left their bills in stacks of unopened post; others have thrown out invoices thinking they were junk mail. One woman simply stuffed her bills under a cushion. Needless to say, these bill-paying 'methods' can be costly.

This chapter provides you with a simple and effective system for paying your bills. Perhaps the tips will make bill-paying somewhat less painful.

## Setting up a household affairs folder

- Visit a stationery shop and buy a ringbinder with different coloured dividers to make a Household Affairs Folder. Here you will store your yet-to-be-billed shopping receipts, your unpaid bills, and your copies of the bills you have paid. After a year store them away in the Household Affairs Folder for that year.
- Mark the outside of the folder with the current year.
- Divide the binder into sections with categories such as: Car, Bank Records, Income Tax, Insurance Records, Medical/Dental, Rates, Receipts, Rent and Mortgage Records, Utilities, Unpaid Bills, and so on according to your needs.

## Sorting bills, receipts, and solicitations

- Keep *shop receipts for items you have charged* in a small envelope within the Receipts section. The envelope keeps everything together for eventual cross-checking with the bill and allows you quickly to find out just how much you have paid for by credit card at any given time.

- When a *bill* arrives in the post, open it. Pull out your receipts and be sure that all charges are correct. If not, you have time to straighten it out before the bill is due. If action is necessary, phone or write to the company. If all is in order, check the due date and put the bill back in its original envelope. On the outside of the envelope, mark the date the bill is due. File it in chronological order in the Unpaid Bills section of your Household Affairs Folder.

- When you receive *solicitations for charitable gifts*, file those that interest you in the Unpaid Bills section as well. (After covering other costs, you will have a better opportunity to evaluate to whom and how much you want to give.)

## Establishing a system

- Assign one member of the family to be in charge of bill-paying. My husband and I take six-month stints at the job, but most families find it works better if just one person pays the bills all the time.

- Choose a set time once a week for bill-paying and allow approximately 15 minutes for it. You may be wondering why you can't do it just once a month. There are three reasons. First, bills arrive throughout the month, and if you've only established one bill-paying period, you may find that you'll end up with charges for late payments. Second, by paying once a week, you can pay closer to the date that the money is actually due. That gives *you* the use of your money for a longer period of time rather than letting the company earn interest on it. And finally, it is the rare chequebook that can withstand one major bill-paying assault. By paying throughout the month you have allowed a little cash to flow in before it needs to flow out again.

- Establish a set place (your desk or the kitchen table, for example) for paying your bills.

- Have on hand a pen, your chequebook, a few extra envelopes, stamps, and your Household Affairs Folder.

# The process

- Remove all the bills and solicitations from the Unpaid Bills section of the folder. Pull out the ones that you need to get in the post soon.

- If you did not do so when the bills arrived, you will need to crosscheck the bill with your receipts. Take out the envelope of receipts from the Receipts section of the folder. For all bills, compare your shopping receipts with the actual charges. Make sure that all amounts charged are correct and that there are no extra charges about which you have questions.

- As you write the cheque, be sure to date it, correctly identify the payee, fill in the correct amount, and sign it with your legal signature. In addition, every cheque should carry some additional identifying information: a cheque to a department store should have your charge account number; a payment for your phone bill should have your phone number; a major credit card payment should have your credit card number.

- When it comes to payments such as insurance, be sure to note your policy number, the type of insurance (car, life, health) and the time period which the payment is to cover on *both* the cheque and in your chequebook. Sometimes the computer continues to spew out bills despite the fact that you've paid them. This record will tell you whether you're up to date on your payments for different policies.

- Mark 'Tax' with a coloured pen by any items in your chequebook which are deductible so that a quick scan of the chequebook will give you accurate records from which to work.

- Once the bill is paid, send off the cheque and the company's portion of the invoice in the envelope provided (or use one of your own, if necessary).

- Mark your portion 'paid' and put the date of payment and the cheque number on it. If you aren't paying the entire amount, note the amount that you did pay. Then transfer your part of the invoice or statement to the appropriate category in the Household Affairs Folder. (Utilities, Medical /Dental, etc.).

- For insurance purposes (see Chapter 19), it is helpful to

create a list of major purchases such as jewellery, cameras, furs, and household items of value, and bill-paying time is a good opportunity to tend to these records. You may want to check with your insurance company regarding what constitutes a major purchase, or perhaps you're comfortable working with a figure such as £200. On a sheet of paper, write 'New Purchases 198__'. As you make purchases throughout the year, note those that are over £200 (or the figure you selected), and after you've paid the bill, take the receipt for each item and store it in an envelope along with your inventory list. These records should be filed in your Cash Receipts file in your filing cabinet for the rest of the current year; at the end of the year they should be moved to your strongbox. The records should be retained for the life of the items.

- Information and receipts pertaining to the purchase of your home and/or any home improvements should be retained until you sell the home; thus it is advisable to move these receipts into a permanent file rather than leaving them in your Household Affairs Folder. After paying such bills, remove these records and receipts and file them in your Housing file in your filing cabinet (see Chapter 10).

- Now take a look at any charitable solicitations you may have received. Do you have £30 to send to XYZ Charity? If so, write out the cheque and send it to them.

- File charitable donation confirmation slips and pertinent correspondence in the Income Tax section of the folder.

- Keep a running total of your bank balance. Too many people enter the amount of the cheque but neglect to do the calculation to keep the total current. This makes it all too easy accidentally to overdraw your account.

- Seal and stamp your envelopes. If they should be posted the next day, put them with your outgoing items near the front door.

## What to do at the end of the year

Your Household Affairs Folder will serve as a perfect record of your expenditures during any given calendar year and should be saved. Here's what to do:

- In early December, buy a new Household Affair Folder.

- At the end of December, take out any materials from the old folder which should be transferred to the new one (unpaid bills, loan information, etc.).

- Close up the old folder and put it in an oversized envelope or expandable folder along with your deposit slips and cheque stubs folder (see Banking) for the year, and any other pertinent information. Label the folder with the appropriate year, and place it in dead storage.

- While some items need to be kept for only three years, tax-related receipts and information need to be kept for six — so I recommend waiting the full six years before cleaning out your Household Affairs Folder.

# 16: Budgeting

For many months I had a client who would frantically call me week after week because she couldn't remember how and where she had spent her money. 'I know I started off with £100 yesterday. Today I only have £10 left. How could I have spent so much money?' Each time we would reconstruct the errands she'd done and the places the money had been spent, and each week there was an explanation; but her feelings of being out of control were so painful that over time she finally adopted a more sensible approach and started budgeting.

How often have *you* said, 'I just don't know where my money goes'?

The purpose of this section is to help you establish a simple record-keeping system that will give you a better understanding of the whereabouts of your money.

## *Setting goals*

- Set a long-term goal. When it comes to budgeting, most people want a long-term reason why they should do it: 'I want to get ahead so that I'm not always worrying about how to pay the next bill . . .'; 'I want to start saving for my children's college education. . .'; 'I want to start preparing for retirement . . .'; 'I want to buy a house in a couple of years . . .' A long-term goal will give you a reason for sticking with budgeting.

- Establish short-term goals, with rewards. Sometimes people make the mistake of setting only a long-term goal. The problem with this is that it's easy to get discouraged − it can take months or a year or more before you begin to reap any rewards from it. Instead, establish short-term goals with rewards: 'If we maintain our budget for two consecutive months, we'll treat ourselves to a special dinner at a restaurant' (one that is within your budget); 'If I save £500, I'll buy myself a new sweater for £35.' Such short-term goals make budgeting easier in the short run.

## Establishing a system

- *Income.* Surprisingly, many people don't know exactly what their actual income is. The following chart can help you document your monthly income (both income and expenses are figured on a monthly basis). Note take-home pay for both husband and wife, part-time income (moonlighting), and all other money your family receives regularly. For amounts that come in annually, such as a company bonus, divide the amount received by 12 to arrive at a monthly figure.

- *Expenses.* Next, you need to determine your expenses. For our purposes, *fixed expenses* will be defined as unavoidable monthly costs, those you must pay each month. *Variable expenses* include items such as clothing, holiday expenses, and entertainment − costs which are often necessary but which you may not incur every month. Note that some expenses might be fixed for one family and variable for another; for parents who work outside the home, child care is an unavoidable expense. If, however, only one parent works and child care expenses consist of paying for babysitting a few times a month, that cost might be considered variable. Be sure to average in quarterly or annual payments such as insurance premiums, and rates. For example, if one of your insurance premiums is £150 per year, you need to set aside £12.50 (£150 divided by 12) in order to cover that expense.

- *Personal allowance.* Note that this is listed as a fixed rather than variable expense. Each family member should be alloted a reasonable amount of discretionary money if family budgeting is to be successful. If you begin to feel deprived, you might be tempted to dip into money you're earmarking for other things. For children, having a personal allowance introduces them to some of the challenges of managing money.

- *Savings.* This is also listed as a fixed expense. For everyone, saving something (even £20 or £25 per month) should be a top priority. Almost everyone encounters a 'rainy day' at some point, so don't put yourself in the position of saying, 'I *wish* I'd saved!' When you pay your rent or mortgage, you should get in the habit of automatically writing a cheque to your savings account. By treating savings as a fixed expense, you can be guaranteed that you'll have money for something special or for when you need it.

● Now work through the following budget, adding items as necessary.

# MONTHLY BUDGET

| Income | | Expenses | |
|---|---|---|---|
| | | ***Fixed*** | |
| Husband's take-home pay | ———— | Housing | ———— |
| | | (rent or mortgate pmts.) | |
| Wife's take-home pay | ———— | Income tax | ———— |
| | | (if not withheld) | |
| Moonlighting | ———— | Rates | ———— |
| Company bonus | ———— | (money set aside for | |
| (as it would average | | annual pmts.) | |
| into monthly income) | | Insurance | |
| | | Household | ———— |
| Dividends | ———— | Car | ———— |
| | | Health (BUPA/PPP) | ———— |
| Interest | ———— | Life | ———— |
| | | Savings | ———— |
| Education | ———— | Gas and electricity | ———— |
| | | | |
| Other | ———— | Utilities | |
| (profit-sharing | | Water | ———— |
| pension, royalties, trust, | | Telephone | ———— |
| etc.) | | | |
| | | Food | ———— |
| | | Transport | ———— |
| | | Child care | ———— |
| | | Medical/Dental | ———— |
| | | Education | ———— |
| | | Debts or loans | ———— |
| | | (car payments, etc.) | |
| | | | |
| | | Personal allowance | ———— |
| | | | |
| | | ***Variable*** | |
| | | Medication | ———— |
| | | Clothing | ———— |
| | | Home maint. & furn. | ———— |
| | | Entertainment/ recreation | ———— |
| | | Domestic help | ———— |
| | | Charitable donations | ———— |
| | | Holiday savings | ———— |
| | | Other | ———— |
| **TOTAL:** | | **TOTAL:** | |

## Identifying trouble spots

- Now that you have one total for your disposable income and another for expenses subtract your expenses from your income to see how you come out. If you're fortunate, your income will exceed your expenses and you will have a 'surplus' which you can divert to savings. However, for many people, expenses exceed income, which means they must trim their budget. For example, perhaps your food budget includes bringing home food from a gourmet take-away shop one night a week. Consider bringing in dinner just once a month until you get expenses more in line with your income. Also review each item under expenses and see where you can save. But be realistic! Don't cut out all money for magazine subscriptions if you have one or two publications you really enjoy — just cut the costs of the ones you don't read so eagerly anymore. We cut down on two subscriptions when my daughter was born because we never had the time to read them anyway, and we knew that extra time was going to be at a premium once we had a new baby!

- If you are significantly overextended, you may need to seek financial counselling or think long and hard about how to bring your life-style more in line with your income.

- Watch your cash. For many people, weekly cash expenditures are a real problem, primarily because they just don't know where the money has gone. . . . Maybe you've allotted yourself £50 personal spending money for the week, but somehow by Friday or Saturday, you're dipping into next week's allotment because you just don't have anything left. Try this: slip an index card into your purse or wallet. Every time you spend cash on an item, note down how much you spend and on what. At the end of the week, most people discover they have a weakness for something which they totally forget about. Perhaps it's paperback books or record albums, or lunch in a restaurant a couple of times a week. Whatever it is, once you're aware that your habit is proving costly, you'll be able to cut back on those expenses *if you want to.*

## Charting monthly expenses

To help you understand where your money goes, use the

following chart to keep track of exactly what you spend each month:

## JANUARY 198—

| Expenses | Date | Cheque No (if applicable) | Amount |
|---|---|---|---|
| *Fixed* | | | |
| Housing | | | |
| Income tax | | | |
| Rates | | | |
| Insurance | | | |
| Household | | | |
| Car | | | |
| Health (BUPA/PPP) | | | |
| Life | | | |
| Savings | | | |
| Utilities | | | |
| Gas and electricity | | | |
| Water | | | |
| Telephone | | | |
| Food | | | |
| Transport | | | |
| Child care | | | |
| Medical/Dental | | | |
| Education | | | |
| Past debts or loans | | | |
| Personal allowance | | | |
| *Variable* | | | |
| Medication | | | |
| Clothing | | | |
| Home maint. & furn. | | | |
| Entertainment/recreation | | | |
| Domestic help | | | |
| Charitable donations | | | |
| Holiday savings | | | |
| Other | | | |

## *Keeping it up*

With some practice, you'll find that budgeting can become a matter of habit, and that paperwork will be unnecessary. Until then, keep a monthly record (like the one above) of exactly what you're spending in each category. Later, a quick glance through your chequebook will show you where the money for that month has gone. And by the way, even cash withdrawals should note: '£30 groceries'; '£20 spending money'.

- Be sure to budget for the unexpected. It's better to have extra money at the end of the year rather than be caught short when extra bills come in.
- Review your budget every six months to be sure it is still serving your needs.
- Keep your goals and your budget realistic, and you'll find that budgeting is well worth the effort.

# 17: Financial Master List

There are two occasions when having a master list of your financial information is especially helpful. The first occurs when certain items are lost or missing (credit cards stolen, personal papers and insurance policies destroyed in a fire).

The second happens in the event of death or incapacity. And of course, at the time of such a stressful event, loved ones should not have to worry about locating items which may be needed immediately (power of attorney, will) and those that will be needed shortly (financial papers, insurance policies).

Here's how to compile such a list.

## Gathering important numbers

If documents are lost, it is much easier to replace them if you have a list of identifying numbers. This information is also helpful to an executor settling an estate. Such numbers should include:

- Bank account numbers; name and telephone number of your banker.

- Each credit card number and the telephone number to call if the card is lost or stolen. (Or register with a credit card service. If cards are lost or stolen you can call one telephone number – the service – and they contact all the credit card establishments.)

- Driving licence number.

- Individual pension plan number; location.

- Insurance policy numbers, the insuring companies, and the name and telephone number of insurance company.

- Savings account numbers.

- Stocks and share certificate numbers (if kept in your possession).

## *Preparing additional information for your executor*

This information should round out the above to provide a complete reference sheet to your financial affairs. Include on it:

- Accountant's name, address and telephone number.
- Employee benefits, the company telephone number, and the extension of the individual in the company who handles benefits.
- Financial obligations, such as your mortgage and any other outstanding loans as well as any money owed to you.
- Investments — list them and the name and telephone number of your broker (who can provide information on short-term investments since it is difficult to keep an up-to-date record).
- Solicitor or person who has power of attorney — name, address, and telephone number of the person(s) who have been given power of attorney and what the power covers (signing cheques, selling property, etc.).
- Properties owned, the locations, and the whereabouts of the deeds.
- Safe-deposit box — its location, an inventory of its contents, and where you keep the key.
- Whereabouts of:
  - ★Personal papers
  - ★Bank records
  - ★Tax records
- Will — location and the name and telephone number of the solicitor who wrote it.

## *Maintaining the list*

- You'll need three copies of your Financial Master List. One copy should be kept in your safe-deposit box; another should be in your Important Documents file; a third should be in your strongbox (see Chapter 20).
- Update the list as needed. Whenever you visit your safe-deposit box, check the contents against the list to make sure it's up to date.

# 18: Investments

If you regularly comb the financial pages checking on the day-to-day fate of your stocks, then you probably have a system for watching your investments. Or perhaps you are more of a dabbler, or if your great aunt Milly left you some stock, and now you *must* become more knowledgeable, you will benefit from using this basic system for monitoring your portfolio.

## Establishing a system

- Have on hand:
  - ★ Pen
  - ★ Paper.
- Gather together any material you have received from your stockbroker. This would include statements, as well as buy/sell confirmations. Because this information needs to be kept with your annual records, it will eventually be stored in the Investments section of your Household Affairs Folder, but first you need to make a list of your holdings. Having these records will save you time when making a tax declaration.
- Establish a separate sheet for each type of brokerage account you have. (In addition to your own account, you may have a joint or custodial account you control.)
- Here's the information you will need to record: name of the stock or bond, the number of shares/amount you own, date acquired, total cost of purchase including commission. When you sell, note the date sold and total sale price. You'll then want to note your profit or loss. A chart might look like this:

81

| Stock | No. shares | Date acquired | Cost or other basis | Date sold | Sale proceeds | Profit/loss |
|-------|-----------|---------------|--------------------|-----------|---------------|-------------|
|       |           |               |                    |           |               |             |
|       |           |               |                    |           |               |             |
|       |           |               |                    |           |               |             |

- If any of your holdings are gifts or inheritances, you'll need to ascertain what date to use as your acquisition date and the amount which should be your cost basis. The executor of the estate or the person who gave you the gift can provide this information.
- Note that if you hold long-term investments (for your children's education, for example), you should indicate the date they will come due. This will aid you in planning and organising for that time.
- If you participate in mutual funds, employee share options, or an investment club, you should track those investments in a similar manner.
- All records of purchases and sales of the same security should be kept together.
- Save all the transaction confirmations you receive, and file them in your Household Affairs Folder under Investments. They will be an important validation of your list.

## Monitoring income

- If the securities are income-producing, you will need to track these payments as well. Some people have the cheques sent to their homes; others have the income deposited directly into their brokerage accounts.
- To monitor income, set up a simple list that notes the name of the company, the amount of the dividend or interest payment, and the date (when you buy or sell a bond there will

be interest income or interest expense on the confirmation which should be included on this list):

| Stock/bond | Date | Div. or int. rec'd | Taxable | Non-taxable |
|---|---|---|---|---|
| | | | | |
| | | | | |
| | | | | |

- Keep this list in your Investment file in your filing cabinet since it is a permanent record you may refer to frequently.

## *Monitoring performance*

- Keep track of the performance of your portfolio regularly. Financial advisers recommend doing it at least quarterly, if not monthly.
- You should also read the financial pages of your newspaper to be aware of fresh information regarding your securities.

| Date | Stock/bond | Orig. cost | Price now | % + or— | Action? |
|---|---|---|---|---|---|
| | | | | | |
| | | | | | |
| | | | | | |

- To see how your investments are doing, note the date and the stock price. Then compare your original investment cost to the current price to see whether you have a profit or loss. Also compare the current price to the price the last time you monitored performance to see how they compare. As you check each stock, make notes as to any action you might want to take (Buy? Sell? Watch closely?).

- Check your investments regularly to make sure they are in line with your financial goals and are performing well for you.

# 19: Personal Property Inventory

If your home were ransacked by burglars or destroyed by fire, would you be able to provide your insurance company with itemised bills of sale (receipts) for your more valuable possessions? For most people, the answer is no.

In this chapter, I will provide you with a system so you will be able to say yes. In addition to creating a record-keeping system for bills of sale, a Personal Property Inventory − which provides a record of your possessions − will help you get the full value from your property insurance should a disaster ever befall your home.

## Taking inventory

- You are going to need to take an inventory of your home, but before doing so, call your insurance company to ascertain what type of information (and proof of possession) is required under your policy.

- Set aside time for this project. Some people prefer to devote a Sunday afternoon to it; others prefer to do it a room or two at a time − a simple room might take five minutes while a more complicated room might take up to an hour. Though the project may seem overwhelming, it will seem to go more quickly if you think of it room-by-room.

- Have on hand:
  - ★Pen
  - ★Pad of paper (or ask your insurance company to provide an inventory booklet − most companies can supply them)
  - ★Camera with several rolls of film
  - ★Strongbox (fire-resistant file box available at most office supply stores). This is a sensible place for storing the Inventory once you've finished it.

- Choose a room, such as the study, to begin. Note down the major items you have there.

85

- After each item note the year of purchase and the price. (If you don't know the exact price, you'll have to estimate.)
- Next, take a photograph of each of the different sections of the room, showing as many items as possible.
- Proceed to the next room, remembering to check kitchen, bathrooms, and hallways for items of value.
- Don't forget drawers. Check each one, and itemise and photograph valuables.
- Items of particular value such as jewellery or furs may need to be covered under a rider to your homeowner's or tenant's policy and will also need to be carefully documented.
- When the film is developed, order two copies of the prints you need. Arrange to have three copies made of the Inventory. One set of photos and an Inventory will be stored in your home strongbox; another set and an Inventory should be stored in your safe-deposit box; the third copy of the Inventory should be kept in your Insurance file in the filing cabinet.

## *Updating the inventory*

If you ever need to make an insurance claim, your agent would much prefer it if you could provide him with sales slips for all the major possessions involved. Thus, receipts or valuations are the key to the future maintenance of your Personal Property Inventory.

- For claim purposes, you need to decide what cash amount constitutes a large purchase. You may want to check with your insurance company, or perhaps you're comfortable working with a figure such as £200.
- If you have not already done so (as suggested in Chapter 15), you will now need to create a list for these items. On a sheet of paper, write 'New purchases 19__' File it in your Cash Receipts file.
- As you make purchases throughout the year, note those that are over £200 (or the figure you selected) on this sheet; after you've paid the bill, take the receipt for each item and store it in an envelope along with your Inventory list.

- On January 1 when you are packing away old household records to make way for new ones, transfer the past year's Inventory list *and the sales receipts* to your strongbox. This will provide a safe place for these documents.

- Create a new 'New Purchases 198__' sheet for the upcoming year. (Put a reminder slip 'Start new inventory sheet; move old one' in your January Tickler File to be sure the job gets done.)

# 20: Safe-Deposit Box and Strongbox

You may *think* you don't need a safe-deposit box.... Your papers are 'fine where they are', and you have the perfect place for hiding your valuables. ... Do you:

- Hide your money in a book?

- Keep money or jewellery in canisters or aluminium foil in the refrigerator or freezer?

- Stash money among the leaves of lettuce?

- Freeze small pieces of jewellery inside ice cubes?

One woman I know is so untrusting of institutions (and people) that she carries her entire savings – thousands of dollars – with her every day!

The problem with all of these methods is that they are unreliable. The best place for important papers and valuables is in a safe-deposit box.

When it comes to having one, there are two main problems people encounter:

- They don't know what to keep in it: 'Should I keep the original of my will there? Do my insurance policies need to be stored in a safe-deposit box?'

- They don't know a good system for keeping track of what is in the box: 'Is my passport there, and where is our marriage licence ... ' 'Did I put my gold pendant watch in the box, or is it missing?'

This chapter will help you organise the contents of your safe-deposit box, and you will never again need to worry about what you're keeping in it.

We'll also talk about strongboxes, and I'll list for you what should be kept there.

## *Selecting what goes in your safe-deposit box*

Anything that is too valuable to be accidentally misplaced or destroyed by theft, fire or natural disaster should be stored in your safe-deposit box. Typical items include:

● Certificates of birth, death, marriage, and divorce.

  ★ A *copy* of your will with a note specifying the location of the original – usually with your lawyer; another copy should be kept in your filing cabinet

  ★ Financial Master List (see Chapter 17) for your executor noting the exact location of important documents; names and addresses of personal and legal advisers (original in safe-deposit box; one copy in Important Documents in filing cabinet; another copy in strongbox)

  ★ Legal documents

  ★ Mortgage papers

  ★ Passports

  ★ Pension plan

  ★ Personal Property Inventory (one copy in safe-deposit box; one copy in file; one copy with receipts in strongbox)

  ★ Stock certificates, bonds and certificates of deposit

  ★ Titles to property (boat, etc.)

  ★ Titles to real estate

  ★ Trust documents.

● In addition, you may choose to store small valuables such as jewellery or valuable collections such as coins and stamps here permanently or while you are on vacation.

## *Box maintenance*

● Make a list describing all items in your safe-deposit box and keep it in your filing cabinet under Important Documents.

● Arrange the contents neatly in the safe-deposit box. Store the documents in clearly labelled envelopes.

● Not even safe-deposit boxes are 100 per cent safe. If the vault is robbed, banks generally do not have insurance covering the contents of safe-deposit boxes. If you are storing items of exceptional value, you may want to take out extra insurance cover for the contents of your box.

- Visit the box at least once a year to check the contents, and update your list as needed.

- Use the annual visit as an opportunity to review items stored there (e.g. read through your will and be certain that it still expresses your current wishes).

## *The need for a strongbox*

A strongbox is a small, fire-resistant file box which can be purchased at most office supply stores. Most strongboxes will survive all but the most devastating fires, so it offers you a relatively safe place to keep important documents that don't really need to be in your safe-deposit box but which would be inconvenient to lose in a fire or other natural disaster. Strongboxes are not burglar-proof, so valuables should not be stored here.

Items you might keep in your strongbox include:

- Financial Master List.

- Personal Property Inventory.

- 'New Purchases' sheets for each year along with appropriate receipts.

- All papers in your Important Documents and Insurance files which would pertain to reconstructing your life after a fire or other property disaster.

# Section 4
## ~
## Household Matters

# 21: In Case of Emergency

Whether it's a power failure or a serious injury, readiness is your best protection when there is an emergency.

## To post:

Post an 'emergency procedures' card by all telephones and near the place you choose to keep your first-aid kit. The card should include the following information (type the names of the places and persons in capital letters to make the card easy to read):

- Address of nearest hospital CASUALTY DEPARTMENT and brief instructions as to how to get there.
- Name and telephone number of family DOCTOR.
- Name and number of nearest NEIGHBOUR who would help.
- Name and telephone number of FAMILY MEMBER (mother, sister) to call for back-up help.
- ADDRESS of your home, in case a flustered babysitter or cleaning person is making the call. (In an emergency, *you* might even forget!)
- If there are children, the card should also include:
    ★CHILD'S FULL NAME.
    ★PARENTS' FULL NAMES and telephone numbers at work
    ★Child's BLOOD TYPE
- Name and telephone number of VET (if you own a pet).
- Family allergies, chronic illnesses (epilepsy, asthma, etc.), and any medications taken regularly which might affect emergency treatment.
- Make photocopies of the above information, and put them in accessible, logical places: One should go in the nappy changing bag; a regular babysitter should have one in his or her wallet; a third should be in your Household Notebook (see Chapter 22). In addition, a supply should be slipped into a

kitchen drawer. A new babysitter should be shown where the emergency numbers are posted near the telephone and also instructed to take a photocopy from the drawer if he or she must leave with the children under emergency circumstances. The address of the casualty department and your child's blood type will be of little use if the sitter doesn't have the information.

## *Additional telephone numbers*

In addition to the emergency numbers suggested above, you should also keep the following on hand in your Resource File (see Chapter 13) under Home Service Resources.

- Telephone number of gas board/electricity board in case of power failure or gas leak.
- Telephone number of appliance repair offices in case of malfunction.

## *Have on hand*

- Fire extinguisher.
- Torch and batteries (check batteries periodically) or lantern.
- Candles.
- Tinned goods.
- Powdered milk.
- One good, easily readable book about first-aid and emergency procedures. You may not have time to refer to it in an emergency, but if you do, it could make all the difference.

## *Courses everyone should take*

Contact your local Red Cross for information about the following:

- First-aid course.
- Infant safety course.

## For children

- Almost certainly, people other than yourself (a friend, grandparent) take your baby or child out of the house occasionally. You can help them be ready for an emergency by preparing an envelope with the following information (print it on the outside of the envelope):

  ★Home and work telephone numbers (do not include addresses for security reasons)

  ★Telephone number and address of doctor

  ★Address of nearest casualty department.

- Place £10 in the envelope (usually enough taxi fare to get to most places in a city) and at least two ten pence pieces for telephone calls. That way you've provided the information (telephone numbers) and the tools (money) a person needs to best cope with an emergency. The envelope should be kept in the nappy or stroller bag and pointed out to anyone who looks after your child.

- All parents would like a way to guarantee that, if lost, their child would be promptly identified and they would be immediately notified. Identification tags are becoming available which can be attached to the tongue of a child's shoes, providing a bother-free way to assure that your child would almost certainly be wearing the label if lost.

## Teach your children

- As soon as possible (certainly by age three), begin training your child to dial an emergency telephone number. Very young children have been credited with saving the lives of others because they knew what to do in an emergency. Help them practice dialling other telephone numbers so they'll be familiar with dialling the phone. Discuss possible scenarios with them in a matter-of-fact way: 'If I fell and hit my head on the bath and didn't get up, what would you do?' Their response should be that they would make the call.

- As soon as possible, teach them their telephone number and address.

# 22: Household — General

Those who say that running a household requires excellent management skills are absolutely right. Family scheduling, inventory management, purchasing, budgeting, performing or delegating tasks, entertaining, long-term planning (e.g. for a holiday or a household move) are all part of a job which should be described as 'household manager'. The person responsible for seeing that everything gets done has as challenging a job as any manager in a business or corporation.

## *Household: establishing a notebook*

To keep track of the 'thousand-and-one' tasks there are to do, I recommend use of a special organisational tool, the Household Notebook. You'll find that having all household-related information neatly collected in one place is a real convenience.

- You're going to need a looseleaf notebook, dividers (you may need as many as 10 or 12 of them), and paper. The size of notebook is up to you. Some people like to use a small, portable notebook so that they can carry it with them; others use a standard large format for home reference. Visit a stationery shop and select the notebook which is right for you.
- The notebook is a perfect spot for lists of things, such as items 'To Buy', 'To Fix', 'To Do', and 'To Call' (see Chapter 39).
- Your Notebook is also convenient for keeping track of housekeeping chores (see below), for emergency lists and numbers (see Chapter 21), and for party planning (see Chapter 34). In addition, the Notebook can be as varied as it needs to be. Simply create categories as they become necessary. If you're redecorating, you may want to create a category for decorating ideas; you can even tape swatches of material and paint there. If you're househunting, you can cut out and save estate agents' particulars in it. You'll find it an invaluable aid in keeping track of a multitude of details.

## Household: general cleaning

Two couples I know once rented a house together for the summer. Both women were fastidious, so it was a perfect match. They tell a story of going on an initial shopping trip together to buy the necessary food and supplies for the house, spending several hours methodically cruising the paper goods, cleaning, and beverage aisles. By the time they got back to the newly rented home, they had spent £100 and had more than enough scouring powder, cleanser, and window polish — but barely enough food for lunch!

The husband of one said he fully understood that he had a problem when he arrived home to discover Meredith on her hands and knees scrubbing out the firewood bin!

While people don't usually aspire to *that* level of cleanliness, most want a tidy home. Here are some suggestions for getting the housework done efficiently.

- Like anything else, housework goes better if there's a plan. using your Household Notebook, set aside three pages for keeping track of housework. On the first, list jobs that need to be done daily; the second page should have items that need to be done weekly; the third should contain major tasks that can be done less frequently.

- Request help from other family members.

- Hire household help on a regular basis; if you can't afford regular help, consider hiring help for a specific task: cleaning the attic, dusting all the bookshelves, and so forth.

- Keeping up with the day-to-day tasks is vital. Most people find that doing one job each day is ultimately less time-consuming than an occasional full day spent cleaning everything:

  ★If it's Monday, it must be laundry day.
  ★If it's Tuesday, it must be vacuuming day.
  ★If it's Wednesday, I need to buy groceries, etc.

- Before starting a task, decide how long you're going to spend on it. If you know that you can vacuum the house in 30 minutes, then that's really not so bad.

- If you work, save low energy tasks for the evening. (One of my students got *all* her house-cleaning done during advertisements on television!) Try to do larger tasks on

Saturday or before you leave in the morning. One working mother I know prepares the family dinner before leaving for the office.

- Do tasks in bulk. Don't get out the iron to press one or two things. Wait until you have a week's worth to do. Just preparing for a chore like ironing takes long enough that you ought to maximise the 'setting up' time.

- Think of how to make chores more convenient. For example, a 12-foot extension cord on your vacuum can greatly reduce the number of times you have to plug and unplug as you clean.

- If you live in a two-level house, keep one set of supplies upstairs and one downstairs.

- When the time comes to select a major chore (clean out attic, etc.), one woman writes various tasks on several slips of paper and draws the 'chore for the day' out of the box. Whatever the slip says is what she will do.

- Organise your spring cleaning (the major tasks listed on page three of your Household Notebook house-cleaning chores) for set times throughout the year. For instance, once in March and again in September, send rugs and curtains out to be cleaned, have floors waxed, and loose covers changed. Set a time every other month to buff the floor and have the windows washed. Once it becomes a routine, a matter of habit, it will get done automatically without your thinking twice about it.

## Household: reducing clutter

'My house is more disorganised than ever,' said a friend one day. When I asked her why, here's what she told me.

It seems that her mother-in-law used to visit very infrequently, which worked out just fine. According to my friend, the woman is a real 'neatness nut', and so whenever she is coming, my friend has a 'stash day'. She empties all the surfaces of desks, tables, and counters into plastic bags (which she neatly labels and stores in the appropriate cupboards — husband's items in this cupboard, etc.). 'When she arrives, I ask only one thing of her — that she doesn't stand near any cupboard door while it's being opened,' continues my friend.

Well, all went well until there were children. Now the mother-in-law visits three and four times a year, and my friend (who now uses babysitters to help with the 'stashing') has quite an accumulation behind all her closed doors.

If you're anywhere near this point, read this section carefully!

- Leave an area as you found it (or better than you found it). If you've been in the sitting room to watch some television and do a few projects, put back the magazines you thumbed through, and return the sewing kit to the drawer where it belongs. Don't leave anything out.

- Insist that family members help control clutter.

- If doing away with the clutter seems too overwhelming right now, start with just one area, such as the front hall. Make it a point to put everything away as you arrive home and see what it's like to experience a clutter-free front hall. Once you've mastered a system for that area, move on to an area such as the dining room. You'll soon see that tackling just one area at a time will help make house-cleaning much simpler.

- Whatever you do, don't tolerate 'messy clutter build-up'. It will multiply before your eyes! Control it before it gets out of hand.

# 23: Cupboards

Clutter and chaos! Most people suffer from it. How often have you resolved that 'as soon as I have the time I'll clean out those cupboards and drawers . . . '?

One day when I was visiting my aunt she asked me to help her reorganise her cupboards. When I said they looked great to me, she said, 'Oh, well, I thought everything was supposed to be hung by length . . . ' I wish everyone was so well organised that 'hanging by length' was their greatest problem!

With a little thought — and some imagination — cupboard organisation can greatly simplify your life. The more organised the cupboard, the more you'll be able to put in it, and the easier the items will be to use. The following tips are designed to help you create your own personal system and to maximise your storage needs.

## Getting started

- Most cupboards can be reorganised in a day or less; however, in order to do it in that amount of time you need to have all the necessary supplies and organisers on hand. Read through the following information. Then devote a couple of hours to planning for your cupboard needs. After you've shopped for the necessary items, you can set aside half a day or so for each cupboard.

- Organisation begins with planning. Go to the cupboard and study its contents. Consider what should and should *not* be stored there. Should your tennis racket really be on the floor of your clothes cupboard? What about the humidifier? Isn't there somewhere else, a more logical place, for it? Note down your space needs on paper. Often it is not so much a matter of how much space you have as it is how successful you are at dealing with what you have.

- Get specific measurements of everything (dresses, blouses, jackets, trousers, shoes, bags) to allow ample room for them. Measure the longest, tallest and widest item in each category of items in determining the amount of space you'll need. Be sure to take into account that you'll be making future purchases.

## *Reorganising*

- Empty the entire cupboard. Weed out items as you go, throwing out or setting aside to donate what you don't want or haven't used in several years  — if you haven't used it in that amount of time, you probably never will.
- Clean the cupboard thoroughly. Vacuum the floor and baseboards, and wipe down the shelves. If you are repainting, use a high-gloss paint or polyurethane for easier cleaning in the future.
- Measure everything carefully before installing adjustable, multi-level rods.
- In homes with high ceilings, the upper reaches of a cupboard can often be fitted with a clothes rod, and it's a perfect spot for out-of-season storage. A stepstool trip up there twice a year allows a complete switch of wardrobe.
- Shelves should be adjustable and designed to serve individual requirements. When the shelves are very deep, consider sliding drawers instead.
- Install a light that turns on when the cupboard door is opened.

## *Keep items visible and accessible*

- Categorise your clothes according to season, type and colour. Items that go together, such as trousers and jackets, should stay together.
- Store the clothes and shoes you wear most often within easiest reach.
- Invest in sturdy, well-made hangers. They'll help your clothes keep their shape longer and make it easier to stay organised. (Don't hang knitwear! Fold them with tissue paper instead.)
- Don't hang up clothes that need mending or cleaning.

Establish a place to put them until they can be taken to the cleaners or mended. That way you'll know that all clothes that are hanging are ready to be worn. (Keep a list of what has been sent out; check the item off as it comes back.)

- Never store clothing in plastic bags. Plastic keeps clothes from 'breathing' and can also cause discolouration. (Plastic bags are also a safety hazard if there are children in the home.) Instead, store clothes in cotton garment bags, preferably ones that are dark-coloured and won't permit light to come through.

- Use boxes for storage, but only if you can readily identify what is in them. Label the box and list its contents.

- Most people store shoes on the floor of the cupboard, but it is better to keep the floor clutter-free. Otherwise, it becomes a sea of junk and collects dust; items stored there can get ruined. It's also one more area that will soon need cleaning out. Shoes should be stored in labelled (or plastic see-through) shoe boxes, on shoe racks, or on shelves.

- Hang hats and small bags on a pegboard with hooks. You may want to bring the pegboard out of the cupboard and use it as a novel room decoration. Arrange the items in an attractive manner. The pegboard display system will also come in handy when coordinating outfits and accessories, or packing for a trip.

- Large handbags can be stored on shelves. (Hanging may cause large bags to droop and lose their form.)

- Stuff hats and handbags with tissue paper to help them keep their shape.

- Belts and scarves can also be hung, or try rolling them up and placing them in conveniently located baskets or bins.

## *The linen cupboard*

- In this cupboard, try rolling your towels, especially hand towels and facecloths. You'll find this method looks neater and saves space.

- When you store linen and tablecloths, put the folded side out so that you take just the item you need. (If the edges are facing out, it's hard to determine how many sheets or towels you're removing.)

- Fold each bed linen set as a unit (flat sheet and pillow cases within fitted sheet) so you pull out a single set each time.
- Stack linen by room: Keep all sheets for the master bedroom together, all sheets for the guest room together, and so forth. The same goes for towels.
- If your bathroom lacks adequate storage, the linen cupboard is a perfect place to keep extra supplies of soap, tissues, toothpaste and the like.

## The front hall

Take a look at your front hall cupboard, the one guests see when you hang up their coats.

- Be sure the floor is clutter-free.
- Buy attractive heavy-duty coat hangers for the cupboard.
- Divide shelves into sections to organise hats, gloves and scarves; or use individual bins and baskets that are easy to reach. Large hats can be stored and protected in hatboxes.
- If you have a great deal of storage up above, consider a curtain which draws across the shelf area to hide the clutter from guests.
- Put a mirror on the inside of the cupboard door for a last-minute check as you go out the door.

## Redesigning

- Decide on the function of a particular cupboard  −  clothing? storage? linen?
- If you're building from scratch, decide exactly where the cupboard should go.
- Will you use doors, shelves, cupboards, pull-out drawers?
- Be specific about the amount of space you need and what you're storing.
- Size up your belongings. Measure *everything* to determine

rod and shelf placement. Ten sweaters? Six bath towels? You need to allot proper space.

- Leave space for future purchases.
- Consider building compartmentalised drawers and shelves for dividing jewellery, belts and lingerie. Pre-plan their arrangement by laying them out and drawing up a blueprint of the space. A carpenter (or you, if you're handy) can take it from there.

## *General*

- Potpourri and sachets add a pleasing touch by scenting your cupboards. (If needed, anti-moth sachets are also available.)
- Remember to put things back where they belong. 'A place for everything and everything in its place' will put an end to the frustration of hunting for something and not being able to find it when it is most needed. Living by this rule will help simplify your life!

# 24: The Kitchen

I remember visiting a client whose kitchen was incredible. I had never seen one so large or beautiful. But what struck me most about it was how much walking you had to do in that kitchen — how much time was wasted going from one place to another. To get from the refrigerator to the sink and then to the cooker — not to mention the detours along the way for a pot here or utensil there — was like taking a walk around the block.

On the other hand, I remember my first kitchen. It was no larger than a cupboard, but it was very compact and convenient. I could stretch out my arm and reach anything. Because my space was limited, I really had to plan its usage: pare down, keep my counter clutter-free, use all my wall space and capitalise on the kitchen organising tricks I knew. But I loved it, and I had many elaborate, smooth-running dinner parties there. The key? Organisation, of course.

When it comes to organising your kitchen, think function, convenience, and space. You need to consider how you most use your kitchen. Are you primarily a baker? If so, creating a baking centre where all ingredients and appliances are within easy reach should be a specific goal. If you love to cook Chinese food, you'll want convenient cutting surfaces and clear work-tops near the stove.

Many of the suggestions apply to re-planning how to use your existing kitchen without major architectural work. However, if you are redesigning, simply use these ideas to help you formulate what your ideal kitchen should be.

## Working with your plan

- Make a list of your specific needs. Note down the ideal areas you'd like to have (e.g. a good food preparation centre, a baking centre) as well as your complaints (rubbish bin too far from main work area; pots and pans too far from stove). If nothing comes to mind immediately, over the next few days note what works and what doesn't as you perform your usual tasks.

- If you are working with a designer, he or she should provide you with a plan for the layout as well as information on materials to be used and anticipated costs. While you'll want to give the designer the go-ahead once you are satisfied with the plan, remain flexible. Sometimes better solutions present themselves as the work moves along.

- Plan how you would like to arrange each area of the kitchen, one section at a time. Assemble the items that will need to be stored there. Before installing any of the suggested space-savers or making any structural changes, place the items in the cupboard and be certain the space is workable for what you have in mind. For example, if you put in cup hooks, will the shelf below be too cramped for the plates you planned to store there?

## General rules

- Store items close to where they are used. Ovengloves should be near the cooker; glasses should be located next to the sink and/or refrigerator; knives near the cutting board, and so forth.

- Similar items (baking needs or serving trays, for example) should be stored together, with the exception of back-up grocery items, which belong in the pantry.

- Frequently used items such as spices or coffee filters should be stored in the most accessible spots. Infrequently used items should be stored in the back of cabinets or up high, but not so far out of the way you forget the item is there.

## Cabinet storage

- The higher your ceiling, the higher you can go. Build cabinets up to the top, and you will get a great deal of extra storage.

- When it comes to deciding where to place an item, consider how often you will need it. In general, remember that lower cabinets should be used for larger, less frequently used items such as pots and pans, while upper cabinets are generally used for glasses and dishes which you may reach for several times a day.

- Widely spaced kitchen shelves are a waste of space when you're storing most things. For storing smaller items, divide the space by building half-shelves in between the larger ones (or you can buy adjustable shelving). If you build, have the shelves made so they are adjustable. That way they can be rearranged according to your needs.

- Sliding shelves (or ones which swing out) can be easily installed and can bring forgotten pots and pans out into the open where they are easily accessible. A lid and tray rack takes care of lid storage.

- Have dividers built into a cabinet to store baking sheets, roasting pans and trays.

- Store bakeware by stacking in order of usage. If you rarely bake pies, put pie pans on the bottom.

- Make use of wire-coated shelf racks for organising dishes, cooking bowls, and the like.

- Mount hooks underneath a shelf inside a cabinet to hang cups up out of the way.

- For everyday use, have glasses and dishes which are designed to stack.

- If your glassware takes up lots of cabinet space, try racks which fasten to cabinet walls or shelves and suspend the glasses from above, leaving enough room for plates, bowls, and so forth, to be stored underneath.

- The back of a door in a cabinet or cupboard can provide convenient storage in what would otherwise be wasted space. Several manufacturers make plastic-coated wire storage items, including baskets and grids with hooks and shelves, which can be used in many combinations and attach to cabinet and door backs.

- You can also buy special organisers, which can be placed on the back of a cabinet door, for storing aluminium foil, waxed paper, plastic wrap, and other such items.

- Under the sink, and on the inside of one cabinet door, attach a storage system for sponges, detergent, scouring powder, rubber gloves and cleaning brushes.

- Perhaps on the inside of the other door, place a rubbish bin with removable liners.

- An awkward corner cabinet can be made accessible by using

a spinning caddy (lazy Susan), which can also be used for storing spices or small jars of baby food, for example.

- If your refrigerator is small, a wire basket in a cupboard provides a cool, dark, ventilated place to keep fresh vegetables.
- Customise your kitchen cabinets. Visit a hardware shop or the kitchen area of a department store and ask about the various kits available to extend kitchen space.

## Drawers

- For organising the silverware drawer, use a plastic cutlery tray. It keeps the drawer neat and slips out easily for cleaning.
- To keep a 'miscellaneous' (corkscrew, mixing spoons, spatula, etc.) drawer in order, use drawer dividers.
- Drawers are also a good spot for storing spices, aluminium foil, plastic wrap and freezer bags.
- Convert a drawer into a filing cabinet for recipes and instruction booklets. If necessary, cut your file folders to fit.

## Work-tops

Your main goal with work-tops is to keep them clutter-free. Here are some suggestions:

- Canisters and cookbooks are frequently found on many kitchen work-tops. Find space for them on a handy shelf instead.
- Put away all appliances which aren't used daily. Mixers, blenders, and most food processors should be stored in a cabinet rather than on the work-top.
- Microwave ovens also take up space. Certain ovens come with a microwave oven above; other styles of microwaves can be mounted under the cabinet.

## Creating extra work space

- If there is space available, consider buying or having built a work table in the centre of the room. It adds more work space, and a shelf underneath can be used for large cookware.

- If you don't have space to add an additional counter permanently, consider building one that flips up (or folds down or slides in) when not in use.
- Build a removable (or sliding) cutting board for the top of a drawer to extend your work area.
- A cutting board that fits across the sink also provides additional work space.

## On-the-wall storage

- For items used frequently or for those for which you simply don't have the storage, consider a grid unit (made of wire on which pans and utensils can be hung from hooks). It's a great decorative item for such cookware as copper pots and very functional as well.
- Attach a wire basket to the wall under the top cabinet but above the counter. It makes a great off-the-counter storage spot for fresh fruit.
- A pegboard with hooks can be a great addition to any kitchen. A large one can be used for storing pots and pans, a smaller one placed above the counter can be used with an 'easel' attachment to hold a cookbook; special prongs can hold a shelf for spices; longer prongs can hold wine glasses.
- Measuring spoons can be hung from cup hooks mounted on a strip of wood which can be hung conveniently near where you do most of your food preparation.
- Consider a wall-mount grip in a cupboard for broom and mop.

## More ways to organise your kitchen

- Evaluate your electrical outlets. Are they well placed for the kitchen projects which require use of an appliance? If not, outlets can be added at a reasonable cost. Ask friends and neighbours for a recommendation, or check the Yellow Pages.
- Consider track lighting directed at work areas.
- For serious pastry-making, a piece of marble built into a counter can make all the difference! Because it stays cool, rolling out the dough is much easier.

- Don't forget the ceiling! A rack suspended from it can provide an attractive and functional way to hang pots and pans.

- Certain commercial products, such as a free-standing metal shelving unit to store food, supplies, bowls, dishes, and so forth, are durable and very functional. Visit a commercial supply house to see what would work for your kitchen.

- Plastic stacking-bin units (with or without wheels and usually consisting of three or four bins) can be a terrific spot to store placemats and ripening fruit and vegetables.

- Store cleaning supplies in a carrying caddy which stores neatly in a cabinet or cupboard, and can easily be moved around the house.

- Towel holders are sometimes a problem, but adhesive-backed ones are now available which can be put up conveniently near the sink; or if you have an appliance near the sink, you might consider a magnetised one.

- Take advantage of new developments in ironing boards, depending on your space requirements and needs.

- Put away tinned goods by category. Label shelves for easy restocking. Put every thing in alphabetical order, including canned goods and spices. It may seem compulsive, but it will make finding things easier!

- When loading the dishwasher, group together items such as forks, spoons, knives, salad plates, glasses, and so forth, to simplify putting them away.

- Since the kitchen generally serves as the family communication centre, establish a message centre there. Prepare a chart such as the following:

| Mum | Dad | Amanda | Elizabeth | Julia |
|-----|-----|--------|-----------|-------|
|     |     |        |           |       |
|     |     |        |           |       |
|     |     |        |           |       |

Take telephone messages and post notes and reminders. This is also where you should hang the family calendar so that all family members can jot down where they will be each day. Encourage them to include phone numbers and appointment times.

● Emergency information should also be posted near the telephone and family message centre (see Chapter 21).

## Common kitchen mistakes people make

● They don't clean up as they go.
● They don't store things in the most logical and convenient places.
● Usable kitchen space is wasted.
● Each activity requires too many steps to get from one place to another.
● They can't 'remember' where things go.
● They have too much clutter around the kitchen.
● They have no inventory system so they are always running out of things.

# 25: The Refrigerator

In your refrigerator do you have:

- Mouldy cheese?
- An unidentified foil-wrapped 'Mystery meat' from who knows when?
- Rotting fruits or vegetables in the crisper?
- Frozen breads and meats of unknown vintage?

Even a refrigerator needs to be managed. By doing so, you'll make meal preparation easier and cut down on wasted foods by using your leftovers efficiently.

## Starting now

- Although many people today have frost-free refrigerators most refrigerators still need to be cleaned out and wiped down regularly. (If your refrigerator is the type which must be defrosted, then now − while you're reorganising it − is a good time to defrost it.) The best time to clean or defrost your refrigerator is when you're low on food. If you're defrosting, perhaps a neighbour will house the remainder of your perishables and frozen items until you're done. Otherwise, you can salvage perishables (not frozen food) by storing them in a cooler with several ice packs.
- If you need to defrost your refrigerator, empty out all the contents and turn it off.
- If yours is a frost-free model, empty the refrigerator one shelf at a time. Wipe down each shelf as you go.
- Throw out undated items, old cheese, half-used tins of tomato paste, opened jars of spaghetti sauce, jam you'll never use, and all the things which have been in your refrigerator too long or will never be used no matter *how* long they sit there.
- Don't forget to take out and evaluate items stored on the door. Door shelves should also be thoroughly cleaned.
- Empty the dairy box and salad drawer. These drawers are generally removable so you can clean them more easily.

• Sort through freezer items. Remember that freezing just slows spoilage — it doesn't prevent it. If you have food in there from who knows when, you'd better start over again. Use a heavy-duty damp rag to wipe down a frost-free freezer.

## Storage tips

• Establish a purpose for each shelf such as one for milk, juice, and other drinks or one for bread, cheese and cold meats.

• Group together similar items.

• Put the items used most frequently near the front of the shelves; those used less frequently belong at the back.

• Date and label *all* home-wrapped items which go in the refrigerator or the freezer. You really won't remember!

• A one- or two-tier lazy Susan can aid in making the back of the refrigerator (or a cupboard) more accessible. Use it to store mustards, pickles, horseradish and the like.

• Eggs stay freshest if kept in their original carton.

• Milk should be stored on the coldest shelf well inside the refrigerator.

• Store refrigerated meat on the coldest shelf.

• Cut up carrots and celery sticks as soon as you buy them, and store them with a bit of water in a plastic container for convenient snacks.

• Ripe fruit should be refrigerated. If you've cut into it, be sure to wrap it well in plastic wrap.

• Always cover and wrap baked goods to keep them from drying out.

• Stack loaves of bread (dated and labelled) in the freezer. (Pre-slice any full loaves you buy for easier thawing.) Then you can thaw slices as needed.

• Once open, freeze nuts in an airtight container.

• Leftovers can be stored in stackable containers, preferably see-through, so you'll know exactly what you've got.

# 26: Supermarket Shopping and Inventory Control

When you're at the supermarket, how many times have you arrived at aisle 9 only to realise that you forgot to pick up ketchup in aisle 5 and cereal in aisle 6? While there's nothing particularly serious about this, it's annoying at the very least, and a waste of time if it causes you to forget items, necessitating another trip to the store.

My personal feelings about supermarkets have made me particularly eager to streamline this part of my life. The moment I walk into most of them, I want to walk right out again. The traffic is worse than rush hour, and the shopping trolleys seem to double as 'dodgem cars'. The personnel rarely know where anything is. To top it off, I have developed an uncanny knack for always picking the longest checkout line.

Here's what I do to accomplish my shopping efficiently.

## Establishing a system

- Plan all your meals at least one week in advance, and note what foods and ingredients you'll need to buy on your next shopping trip. You don't want to find yourself without tomato paste if you were planning to feed the family lasagna.

- Make and keep handy a list of ingredients for your most frequently-prepared recipes. Then if you want to make Chicken Tetrazzini, you have a convenient list of all the items you need.

- Plan to double up on cooking so you can freeze a complete dish for another night. Take this into account as you consider grocery needs. Making extra sauce can add zip to leftovers!

- The key to organised grocery shopping is a good list. Take five to ten minutes to work out the layout of your supermarket. Or next time you go, take a pencil and paper and note down the general categories in each aisle. Start with the aisle where you generally begin your shopping. This

way your list will tell you what you need in the correct
sequence: Aisle 1 has paper goods, and your list will note first
that you need napkins and paper towels, and so on. Here is a
sample list. This list is alphabetical, which may be more
convenient for people who shop at a variety of stores.

| GROCERY LIST | | |
|---|---|---|
| Baked Goods | Frozen Foods | Misc. |
| Dairy | Fruits | Paper Goods |
| Drinks | Household Cleaning Items | Staples/Seasonings |
| | Meats and Fish | Tinned Goods |
| | | Vegetables |

- Once this chart is drawn up, make photocopies of it to use on
  future shopping trips.
- Choose a spot in the kitchen where you can conveniently
  keep your list and a pen or pencil.
- On the list, record *everything* you need — from the special
  ingredients for a new recipe to the paper napkins you buy
  every week. If you don't write down each item as you think of

it, you will eventually forget to pick up something you 'always buy'.

● Teach family members to record all their grocery needs.

## *Shopping*

● Shop during periods of least activity, preferably when the shop is fully stocked. For example, Monday morning is a poor time for shopping in most stores because the new deliveries are arriving and the aisles are crowded with boxes as the staff tries to re-stock after the weekend. Mid-morning or mid-afternoon might be a good time to shop. You can ask the manager when the store is not busy or experiment by going at different times.

● Buy in bulk or in economy (giant) size. Not only will you save money, but you'll be able to shop less frequently. Sometimes the butcher will give you a discount for buying an entire side of beef and let you take it home as needed.

● Take advantage of special offers. If tuna is priced at a discount, buy ten tins instead of one.

● Some people like to minimise the number of trips they make to the shops. Particularly if you have specialist shops where you pick up fresh items such as meat, bakery goods, and fruits and vegetables, you may be able to shop for staples every other week or even once a month. The trick is to buy all your supplies in multiples. For example, you may need to buy three boxes of the family's favourite cereal and eight rolls of paper towels if you hope to go a month without having to do a major shop. People with home freezers can reduce the number of times they have to shop for meat by buying in bulk here, too.

## *At home*

● Establish a pantry area (even if it has to be a cupboard outside the kitchen) for storing back-up items. Both on the regular kitchen shelves and in the pantry, organise shelves by categories (all tinned goods together, all baking supplies together, etc.).

● Once home, re-wrap meats in appropriate portions. Wrap

some for individual-sized servings in case you're cooking for only one person some night. Label and date them.

● When freezing, always label and date both new purchases and leftovers.

## Inventory control

● Keep a back-up supply of all items. That way when you reach the end of the sugar, for example, you'll open up the extra bag and then add sugar to your next shopping list.

● Teach family members to be diligent about jotting down items when you are low — not out.

## Recipes

● Buy photo albums with plastic pages that tear back so that recipes can be mounted. Buy different coloured books — use one for desserts, one for main courses, and so forth.

● Make notes on recipes such as 'use less salt', 'serves — people', 'cook a little longer'.

# 27: The Laundry

My sister has two sons and recently married a man who has a son of his own. I happened to be there the day they finished doing their first joint laundry. My sister simply looked in horror at a table with piles and piles of underwear and at least two dozen pairs of dark socks. 'Ronni,' she said to me. 'There's got to be an organised way to do this.'

While most of us learn what we need to know about dark loads and light loads and washing towels separately when we first move away from our parents' home, no one gives much thought as to how doing the laundry can be simplified or − in the case of a large family − better organised for speedier sorting.

## Before you wash

Extra care before putting clothes into the washing machine will save you effort in the long run:

- Re-attach loose buttons and do any mending before the item is washed, or the stress of going through the laundry may make the problem worse.
- Remove unwashable items such as belts, shoulder pads, and any ornamentation.
- Turn clothing right side out. It makes for easier folding once the clothes are dry.
- Turn pockets inside out and turn down the cuffs. Brush out sand, lint and dirt.
- Close zips, fasten hooks, and button up for easier folding afterwards.
- To prevent tangling, tie sashes.
- To save on hand washing, use a lingerie bag for delicate underwear.
- Pre-treat stains or pre-soak badly soiled items.

## Simplify

- To streamline doing the laundry, you want to do it as seldom as possible but often enough to keep everyone's drawers well stocked with clothing. Some people can wash as seldom as once a week; others must do it three or four times a week.

- If you note that there is really only one reason (say, fresh underwear) which makes frequent washes necessary, consider buying extra pairs. If you don't run out of anything else, there's no sense in washing for just one type of clothing.

- In these days of heightened time-consciousness, many people have taken to doing hand laundry in the shower. It makes perfect sense. During the minute or so you would normally luxuriate in the warm spray, you can rinse out a couple of items. Try it!

- When putting laundry away, group together items by the room where they belong: stack them in the laundry basket in order of which room you will visit first (top) and which you will go to last (bottom).

## Organising for the larger family

- As suggested throughout the book, colour-coding can be a real aid. By assigning each family member a colour, it can simplify the sorting of some items of clothing (children's pyjamas and underwear) as well as bath towels and facecloths. For bedding, have sheets easily identifiable, such as by using different patterns for each bed so there's no confusion about what goes where.

- Have different laundry hampers for different members of the family. When you wash, do an entire load of only one person's clothes or combine the clothes of family members which are easily distinguishable from each other.

- Or use a laundry pen (use appropriate colours for each family member) to identify family members' similar belongings. Make a mark on the tag large enough so that it is noticeable at a glance.

- Purchase an assortment of baskets – one for each family member. Label and use it for that person's laundry. As soon as they are old enough, encourage your children to pick up their own basket and put their laundry away.

# 28: The Medicine Chest

Let's imagine you have a cold. If you were to go to your medicine chest, how many cold remedies would you have on hand? If you're like most people, you have tablets you purchased when you got sick on holiday, capsules you bought one day at work, a couple of liquid decongestants from who knows when, and some loose foil-packs of pills (without boxes and therefore without brand names and expiration dates) from some long-forgotten cold.

Now suppose you've cut your finger and need some type of antibiotic ointment to put on it. Do you have any? If so, it's probably in an old crumpled tube from five or six years ago, and most of the cream is probably dried out.

In many of the homes I visit, people seem to 'collect' medicines. They suffer a minor illness, buy the latest remedy, take what they need, and store the remainder of the liquid or pills in the medicine chest for use 'the next time I'm sick . . . ,' but the next time, some other remedy seems more appealing.

Neglecting to organise this part of your life can sometimes be dangerous. I'm sure you've heard stories of people who have got up in the middle of the night for an aspirin and have accidently taken some other type of pill. A woman once told me about a time she had something in her eye; she got out what she thought were the eyedrops – and ended up putting nosedrops in her eye instead. Fortunately, no harm was done.

What people need to do is take stock of their medicines, throw out what isn't needed, organise what is, and make a shopping list for first-aid supplies they really ought to have on hand. That's what we'll do now.

## Taking stock

- Spread out all the items from your medicine chest.
- Old prescription medicines (unless they are for a chronic problem or a recurring ailment such as an allergy) should be thrown out – flush them down the toilet so that a child or pet won't retrieve them from a waste-paper basket.

119

- Check expiration dates on all over-the-counter medicines and those that have expired should also be flushed down the toilet.
- Dispose of all over-the-counter medications whose exact use you don't remember and those you don't expect to need again.
- Age and exposure can cause medicines to change, so discard most items over a year old.
- Anything without a label should be thrown away.
- From this time forth, label all medicine you purchase with the date of purchase and what it was for. (How often have you found an old tube of skin cream and can't remember whether it was for a cut or a rash?)
- All prescriptions should be labelled with the type of drug, the date, the person's name, and the instructions. If your pharmacist has not provided that information, add a label of your own.

## *Organising your medicines and supplies*

- Wipe down the bathroom medicine chest. The items you keep here should be things you use daily — toothpaste, deodorant, comb, brush, razor. Because heat and dampness make medicines age faster, the bathroom is not the best place to store medications.
- Also select and clear out another space where you can store the rest of your medicines and first-aid supplies. Be sure the space is well lighted so you will not mistake one medicine for another. If you have children in the household, select an inaccessible cabinet that can be locked.
- Before you start putting things away, establish categories of items and label shelves in the bathroom and in the place you've chosen to keep medicines accordingly ('Hair Care', 'Skin Care', 'Daily Medicine'). You'll be able to find things much more quickly and easily — and it will be much more difficult to mistake the nosedrops for eyedrops because you'll have two different spots for them.
- If you have many items to store, buy a lazy Susan for convenient storage of frequently used items.
- Buy a first-aid box so that all emergency supplies can be kept handy in one place.

- Clean out your medicines annually, throwing out anything you haven't used in the past year. Re-stock on first-aid items you might need.

## Safety tips

- If you have children, buy bottles with childproof caps, but keep in mind that 'child resistant' does not mean it's truly tamper-proof.
- Keep all medicines in their original containers to avoid having someone mistake one medicine for another.
- Read all labels carefully and administer exactly as directed. At night, turn on a light to make sure you have the right medicine and to see that you are measuring accurately.
- After using a medicine, recap it immediately.
- Always return supplies to storage immediately after use.
- Before purchasing over-the-counter items, ask your doctor for recommendations.

## First-aid supplies to have on hand

- Epsom salts.
- Antibiotic ointment or spray to prevent infections in cuts.
- Antiseptic.
- Assorted Band-Aids, butterfly bandages, and a sterile roll of gauze with adhesive tape; scissors to cut tape.
- Burn ointment or spray.
- Baking soda for insect stings, heat rash, or itching.
- Calamine lotion for bites, sun burn and minor rashes.
- Thermometer.
- Petroleum jelly.
- Eyewash and cup.
- Sterile cotton.
- Tweezers for removing splinters.
- Sunscreen.
- Insect repellent.

● Elastic bandage.

## *Basic over-the-counter medicines to have on hand*

● Aspirin or paracetamol.
● Antacid.
● Anti-diarrhoea medicine.
● Antihistamines for allergic reactions.
● Laxative or stool softener.
● Nasal spray.
● Oral decongestant.

# 29: Hiring Household Help

Even if you're an executive at the office, it's often hard to be a boss in your own home. Whether the person you hire is to be a cleaning person or a babysitter, he or she is likely to arrive some times when you're still in your dressing gown, or be there on days when you're feeling sick or down — not exactly a prime moment to be conveying the image of an employer.

When my baby was about eight months old, I set about hiring a babysitter, and I had anything *but* beginner's luck. I set aside an afternoon to be home for interviews, but no one I expected showed up: One woman *forgot*, another misunderstood, and a third got lost. A fourth did come, but she wasn't the woman I'd expected. The woman who came for the job couldn't speak a word of English; the woman I had interviewed and loved on the telephone was her friend who had agreed to make the introductory phone call for her!

I was so discouraged I gave up for a while. Then one day, my old sitter, who had to leave for medical reasons, called me with a recommendation. The person she recommended was perfect!

The best way to approach this task is to hire as a professional would and then do all you can to maintain a good relationship.


## Defining the job

Before you go about looking for the perfect person to solve your problems, you need to make some decisions:

- Think through the job. Decide the hours you will want someone.
- List the duties to be performed.
- Make a list of the qualities and skills you'd like this person to have. Ironing skills? Ability to follow a recipe? Kind and loving with children? Likes pets?
- Will you need this person to travel with you on business or on holiday?
- Talk to friends and relatives about salary, benefits and

holidays, and decide how you want to handle them based on the type of job you're offering.

● Decide whether you mind if a person smokes.

## Starting the search

● Recommendations are the best way to find good household help. Ask friends and family to keep their ears open. You may hear about a friend of a friend who is looking for work.

● Contact agencies.

● Put ads in newspapers. Spend enough money on an ad so you can be very specific about your needs (time availability, non-smoker, driving licence, etc.). That way the majority of calls you get will be from people who meet those criteria. Generally an area will have a specific newspaper where everyone advertises for household help. Ask around so you can advertise in the best place.

● Watch for notices on noticeboards at the local newsagent or launderette.

## Pre-screening

Especially if you've put in an advertisement, you're going to need a method for deciding which of the callers you want to see in person.

● Make up a questionnaire and photocopy it, leaving copies by each telephone with a pen or pencil. The form should have space for a person's name and telephone number, previous employment, your general feeling about him or her ('sounds cheerful', 'English not terrific'), and any point you specifically care about (i.e. non-smoker, likes pets, willing to travel with you and baby if necessary, will work overtime). Try to clarify by phone whether the person fits your basic needs. There is no sense in interviewing a smoker if you *must* have a non-smoker. Or why bother to see someone who won't work overtime when that's something you occasionally need?

● Look for good language skills (at least good enough to communicate with you), general enthusiasm for the job, and positive attitude. In the conversation you should:

★Re-emphasise the days and hours of the job. (Many people who will be calling are working from a list and aren't necessarily sure whom they've called.) Ask about the person's availability during those times.

★Go over job responsibilities, and the necessary skills.

★Clarify any of the above-mentioned requirements.

★Ask about the person's most recent job. Why is he or she leaving?

★Does the person have references? (You don't need them just now, but be sure the person has them.)

★Describe where you live and ask how the person plans to get there.

● If you have a positive feeling based on this short conversation, schedule an interview. Or you may prefer to take the person's name and number until you decide on the top three people you want to see. When you set up the appointment with potential helpers, be sure to do the following:

★Emphasise that it's very important they phone if they can't make it.

★Be sure to get their telephone number so you can call and cancel if you need to. Or ask them to call you in advance of the appointment so that you both can confirm.

★Give them explicit directions as to how to get to your home.

## *The interview*

Most people are very nervous at interviews, so don't discount them immediately just because they seem ill-at-ease. Begin by again describing the job so they have time to collect their thoughts. During the course of the interview, you will want to ask:

● Are you currently employed, and if so, what kind of work are you doing? How long have you been employed there?

● Why are you dissatisfied with your current job?

● What have your experiences been with __? (infants, teenagers, cooking, cleaning, elderly, parties, etc.)

● What tasks did you do at your last job?

● What other responsibilities do you have? (Here you're looking for whether they may have to take their mother to the doctor once a week — or anything which might mean they would have difficulty getting to the job regularly.)

● Are you planning to move in the near future? When? (There's little sense in training someone who cannot stay long.

● Do you have any holiday plans?

● What don't you consider part of the job?

● Any special things I ought to know about you? (bad back, dislike pets, allergies).

● Put together some 'what if' questions to get a sense of how he or she would handle certain situations. If you're hiring someone to care for your elderly mother ask questions like, 'What if my mother fell but refused to let you take her to the doctor?' Or for a babysitter: 'How would you discipline my child if he ran out into the street before you said it was time to cross?' Or: 'What would you do if there was lots of laundry to be done, but the baby cried every time you put her down?'

● Are you willing to follow a checklist of daily tasks? (Show him or her one.)

● If he or she is to live in, show the person the room where he or she would sleep.

● Check work permits.

● Be sure to specify days off, pay, holidays, and benefits at the interview.

● If the person is to care for children or the elderly, leave him or her alone with them for a little while. You can wander in and out of the room or eavesdrop to get a sense of how the person handles things. Trust your gut response.

## *Checking references*

Do follow up references. It can save you a lot of trouble in the long run if you've verified the person's qualifications. Ask:

● How long has he/she been with you?

● Why did he/she leave?

● How well did he/she follow instructions?

● Could he/she think quickly in an emergency?

● Was he/she responsible, and did he/she use common sense?

- How well did he/she get along with family members? Was he/she chatty? Did he/she make herself invisible?
- For childcare: how did he/she spend time with your child(ren)? Was he/she particularly good with one age or another? With one type of activity or another? Did your child(ren) like him/her?
- Is there anything I should know about him/her − positively or negatively?
- Did he/she ever do something with which you totally disagreed?
- Was he/she punctual?
- Do you have any advice for us in working with him/her?

## *Working together*

- Once the person has agreed to work for you, go over once again what the pay, holidays, benefits, system of raises, and sick leave arrangements are.
- Establish exactly what the job is. Discuss any peculiarities of yours, such as 'I can't stand finding dishes left in the sink . . .' Or: 'Please be sure the baby's room is tidied up before you leave . . .'
- Discuss expectations, hours, punctuality, and the use of the telephone and television.
- Show the person the appliances and how they operate. (If necessary, compile a How to Operate manual.)
- Specify items not to be touched or cleaned.
- Ask him/her about foods he/she likes and any special dietary needs.
- Buy any needed items if the helper is to live in.
- Set up a probationary period.
- Write out instructions and set up tasks to be done daily, weekly, biweekly.
- Arrange PAYE payments, insurance.
- Keep accurate records of sick days and holidays so that you have a tabulation of what has been used and what hasn't.
- Just as you expect your helper to be punctual, you should be

as well. If you've said you'll be home at 6 o'clock, then you should be there by then 99 per cent of the time.

● Keep the relationship professional. Mild interest in your helper's personal life is fine; don't try to become his/her friend.

## *Additional tips for working with a child-minder*

● Discuss child-rearing practices.

● Establish a regular time each week when you can discuss how things are going. Perhaps you can come home 15 minutes early (or leave a little later) one day a week.

● Keep in mind that your child's needs will change and what used to be a two-hour nap may now have shrunk to one hour. Realise that the child-minder may need some increase in his/her other responsibilities because of that.

● Have neighbours keep a watchful eye, and you should occasionally come home earlier than usual just to see how things are going.

# Section 5
## ~
# Main Events

# 30: Preparing for the Painters

If you think getting ready for the painters is going to be bad, consider the plight of my neighbour. One evening about five years ago, she rang our doorbell. She was exhausted and in a real dither about getting ready for this 'monumental' task, which was taking place the next day. When we went next door, the only thing that had been moved in preparation was an extensive collection of beautiful, delicate glass bottles! It had taken her so long just to do this that she hadn't even begun to prepare the rest of her home!

Some people say that having your home painted is worse than moving, and they may be right. Certainly having to pack up all your belongings and stash them in the centre of a room is a time-consuming process. However, if you can keep in mind how beautiful a new colour scheme and a freshly painted room will look, the nuisance of having to prepare for it won't seem as bad.

## Choosing a painter

- Get recommendations from friends. Ask to see the person's work, if possible.
- Get estimates from at least three painters.
- Ask prospective painters:
  - ★ Who will actually be doing the work? Himself/herself? An assistant? Will the same person be there throughout the job?
  - ★ How will the walls be prepared?
  - ★ Who will order and pick up the paint?
  - ★ Is paint included in the price?
- Show the painter the space that is to be painted, asking if he or she foresees any problems.
- Make sure the person has the proper insurance.
- Check with previous clients as to whether the person stayed on schedule, stuck to his/her price, and was pleasant to have around.

- Once you've selected a painter, go over everything step by step. Make sure the person cleans up each night so you can still live in your home.

- Prepare a room-by-room checklist before the job begins. (How will the painter protect items such as doorknobs and switch plates? Should you remove them? Or will the painter?)

- Work out a pay schedule consisting of a deposit and payment of the balance. Some workers request a midpoint payment, but specifying what is 'halfway' can pose a problem.

- Draw up a written agreement that is very specific.

## *Choosing a colour*

- Collect swatches of wallpaper, pillows and upholstery fabric to take to the DIY shop.

- Initially, shop for a general colour without worrying about the exact shade.

- Once you've selected the basic colour, buy that shade and two others — the immediate lighter and darker shades. Buy the smallest tins available. That way you can test the paint in various lights. (To avoid a potential problem because of mislabelling, ask the merchant to open the tin and show you the paint so you don't end up at home with the wrong colour.)

- Rather than spending considerable energy trying to find a perfect match for a specific colour, let the merchant mix one for you. Generally it only costs more for the first tin, since the formula is then known.

- Choose a finish that is easy to wipe clean, such as a gloss.

- If you're picking up the paint, ask the painter how much you'll need.

- If the painter picks up the paint, be sure he or she does a test patch.

- Label paint tins according to room colour.

- Keep a record of the paint used for each room. Note the colour, formula, brand and finish. File this information in your filing cabinet or in your Household Notebook (see Chapter 22).

## Preparing for the painters

- Get hold of dustsheets to cover and seal furniture. You'll need tape, too.
- If cupboards are to be painted, clean them out. Borrow clothes rails (ask friends and neighbours), and gather boxes (from supermarkets) for temporary storage.
- As you go through your cupboards, pull out items you no longer want. Give them to charity.
- Take down curtains and send them to be cleaned.
- Send rugs out to be cleaned.
- Protect hardware. If the painter is not going to mask it or remove it, you should put each unit (i.e. one switch plate and accompanying screws) in a plastic bag and label it. Keep all hardware and decorative switch plates together in a box to avoid hunting for them later.
- Put the furniture in the middle of the room, cover fully with dustsheets, and tape down to the floor.
- If the paint job is complicated, draw a plan and code it. Put numbers on the wall and label each paint tin accordingly. This lessens the chance of error.
- Have the living room done first. It's usually the largest room in the home and when it's finished, you can store things from other rooms there while they are being painted.
- Keep available all the things you'll need (appointment book, outfit for the next day) so you won't have to dig for them.
- Make alternative meal plans for the day the kitchen is being painted. The family can have cold cereal for breakfast for a few days; a toaster, a hot plate, an electric kettle, and a cooler kept cold with cold-packs (available at hardware stores) will allow you to prepare simple meals.

## Afterwards

- Return clothes to cupboard.
- Move back furniture.
- Re-install doorknobs, fixtures, switch plates, shelves, brackets, etc., and hang pictures.

- Return clothes rods.
- Clean windows.
- Get rugs back from cleaners.
- Get curtains back from the cleaners and hang them.
- Clean your home once the job is over, but don't do an extensive job until you're *sure* the painters are finished!

# 31: Moving

Whether it is across the country or just next door, moving is a major undertaking which requires a great deal of planning and hard work.

People suffer from various moving miseries: Some are still knee-deep in boxes months after a move is over; others never do unpack some of the things they moved with; still others *intend* to unpack efficiently, but become overwhelmed when faced with a new living room full of boxes marked 'General' and 'Miscellaneous'. I've never heard anyone say, 'I loved moving and can't wait to do it again!'

Moving should not be thought of as one major task – but many small tasks instead. Use this list and check off each task as you accomplish it; you'll soon see that by breaking down the move into parts, it *can* be managed and it *will* happen.

## As much in advance as possible: to do

- Get recommendations about removal firms and/or check the Yellow Pages. Have two or three come to your home for a quotation. Before they arrive, you'll want to have a general idea of what goes and what stays. If an entire bedroom set is to be given away, you won't want the cost of moving it taken into account in the overall estimate. Local moves are generally charged by volume and mileage; long-distance moves are usually based on the weight of the shipment, the miles it will be moved, and the size and number of packing cartons and services you'll need.

- When the removal firm arrives, you'll want to learn the following:
  - ★Estimated moving costs
  - ★How movers will pack fragile items
  - ★Provisions of the contract
  - ★Insurance coverage (which you may need to supplement)

- Ask the movers if they will help you disconnect the washer and drier, cooker, refrigerator, freezer, television set and

134

aerial. You'll want to know now if you need to make other arrangements.

● Carefully read the bill of lading (the contract which outlines the terms of your move).

● Consider what work might be done in your new home prior to your arrival. You can probably arrange with the owners for a designer or an architect to make a visit there. If the home will be vacant for a few days or weeks before you arrive, you may be able to get some construction or decorating out of the way. Consider, too, whether a cleaner or window cleaner should come in before you arrive.

● You don't want to move what you don't want, so start taking stock of all your belongings. Sort everything into four groups:

★Items to go with you
★Items to give to friends or relatives
★Items to give to charity
★Items to throw out (Don't insist that your children throw things out − this will only make the move more difficult.)

● Start collecting packing materials. The local off-licence or supermarket may be a good source of boxes; better yet, borrow boxes from the removal company. You'll also need twine and tape. Newspaper makes the best packing material but can soil your belongings.

## *Four weeks in advance: to do*

● Begin sorting through your post to make a list of places you'll need to notify regarding your change of address. Note magazines to which you subscribe, credit card companies, department stores where you have accounts, and so forth. Most can be notified by filling out the change-of-address section of a regular statement. Notify all other companies and agencies by letter (photocopies of a form letter you draw up will be fine), or use the post office's standard change-of-address cards. On your list, note the date you notified each person or place. (At a later date, you will notify the post office about forwarding your mail.)

● Confirm packing and moving dates.

- Begin to use up food from the refrigerator and freezer, and only restock with what you'll need during the next month.

## Four weeks in advance of a move to another town or city: to do

- Make whatever travel plans are necessary. Do you need reservations? Will you need to stay in a hotel the night after your belongings are packed? Will you need hotel reservations?
- Make travel arrangements for pets. Ask your vet about animal tranquillisers, and be sure all vaccination papers are in order.
- Notify schools.
- Close local accounts.
- Return all you've borrowed (including library books), and collect what you've lent.

## Four weeks in advance: packing tips

- Start packing items you're not using regularly such as good china, out-of-season clothing, and the contents of your attic and basement.
- Clean items before packing to save time when unpacking.
- If possible, send carpets, curtains and quilts to be cleaned and have them delivered to the new address. Keep a list of all that is sent out so you can be certain everything comes back.
- Keep things that belong together in the same box: pans with their lids, stationery with envelopes, coffee pot lead with coffee pot.
- Fill all boxes to the top so that items won't bounce around.
- Try to distribute the weight within a carton evenly.
- Use bedding and towels to cushion the contents of some of the boxes.
- Arrange to take houseplants with you, as removal firms will

generally not be responsible for them. If you can't, you'll need to give them away.

- Pack books flat so their spines don't break, and put them in smaller cartons so they won't be too heavy. Add additional packing material to empty corners so the books won't slide around. It is best to pack in the same carton books that will be shelved together.

- Records should be stacked in small cartons and labelled so the removal people can store them in the coolest part of the truck.

- When packing lamps, remove bulbs before wrapping the base in a towel or blanket. Shades can be nested inside one another and packed in a separate box. Use packing material (not newspaper) to fill in extra space.

- Don't add heavy linen to drawers in furniture. Leave chests and desks as they would be normally.

- Consider having the removal people pack kitchen and fragile items. (Some will not take responsibility for items they have not packed.) Otherwise, fragile items and all dishes should be individually wrapped using newspaper or paper towels. Cushion them well.

- Leave rugs, pictures and mirrors in place. The removal people are best prepared to pack and wrap these.

- Hanging clothes are best moved in the removal firms wardrobe cartons. Use these so that you don't have to pack your clothes.

- Fold curtains and linen so they can be draped over a hanger. Then they, too, can be moved in a wardrobe carton.

- Provide each child with a moving box for special treasures. If driving to your new home, consider taking these with you. If that is impossible, label it 'LOAD LAST, UNLOAD FIRST'.

- Establish a box for those items you will need throughout the move: tickets, driving itinerary, important papers, keys to the new house, jewellery, and so forth. Keep the box handy so you can add to it as needed.

- In another box labelled 'LOAD LAST, UNLOAD FIRST', put clean bed linen and towels so they will be accessible as quickly as possible once the removal van arrives at your new home.

- Also put together a survival kit with a hammer and screwdriver, tape, scissors, lightbulbs, a first-aid kit (including children's and adult aspirin, Band-Aids, antiseptic, tweezers, clean needle, cold tablets, and medicine for an upset stomach), paper plates, cups and napkins, plastic tableware, a small saucepan, instant coffee or tea bags, snack food, tin opener, paper towels, toilet paper, detergent, sponges, plastic rubbish bags, and dishcloths.

● Number each box, and then label it as to its contents and the room where it will go. Also note the information on a separate sheet of paper; if you discover that Box 33 is missing, you'll automatically know it had living room lamps in it.

● Dispose of all flammables, such as cleaning fluid, paint and aerosol cans. Drain petrol-powered equipment. The removal people will not take these things.

## *Two—three weeks in advance: to do*

● If you're driving to a new area, have the car serviced for the trip. Check oil, water, battery and tyres.

● Deliver or have picked up the items you plan to give to friends.

● Arrange to have all services disconnected at your old home *after departure* (plan the disconnection date for later than your moving date so you won't be without services), and instruct the companies as to where the final bill should be sent. Disconnect:

  ★ Gas/electricity
  ★ Water
  ★ Telephone

● Notify above services of the date when you'd like service to start in the new location. (Have the telephone in service at least one day prior to the removal van's arrival.)

● Contact the following home services to let them know of your departure:

  ★ Laundry
  ★ Milk
  ★ Newspaper

  Also notify the appropriate places when to start service in your new home.

- Call your insurance company for policy changes. Also discuss any special coverage which might be necessary during the move.

- Arrange for the plumber or the appropriate service repairperson to install your appliances.

## *One week in advance: to do*

- Pick up any items you might still have at the cleaners, laundry, or repair shop.

- If you're moving to a new area, go to the bank to take care of the following:

  ★ Ask the bank to transfer accounts or arrange for a letter of credit to facilitate establishing an account in your new area.
  ★ Ask the bank to transfer the contents of your safe-deposit box if you have one, or withdraw the contents of the box yourself and get the box released.
  ★ Withdraw sufficient funds to cover your expenses until you reach your destination.
  ★ If you know exactly how much the move is going to cost, arrange for cash, money order, or certified cheque to pay for it.

- Arrange for the forwarding of post by the post office (what you've done earlier is to notify regular subscriptions and correspondents; now you need to arrange for the post office to send on whatever post still comes to your old address) by filling out the standard change-of-address form.

- Send address change to your friends. Include your new telephone number.

- Arrange for someone to look after the children. While it's a good idea for children to be at home on moving day, make someone else responsible for their well-being.

- Confirm appointments if needed with the cleaning team, or the window cleaner.

- For a long-distance move, pack suitcases with the clothing and items you'll need during the move.

- Mark 'DO NOT MOVE' on any items you plan to take with you.

## Two days before

- Tape shut the tops of bottles and spillable items.
- Remove window coverings (curtains, blinds, rods) and take down any special light fixtures which were not included in the sale of the house and which you plan to take with you. Removal firms do not routinely perform such tasks.
- Don't pack perishables.
- Type out directions to your new home for the removal people.

## Day before (packing day)

- Empty and defrost the refrigerator and freezer. Let them air for 24 hours. Place baking soda inside to deodorise.
- When the removal people arrive to pack any items you've requested, point out fragile items as well as items not to be moved.
- As they pack, work with them by quickly checking the contents of each packed box. Label it according to its new location (master bedroom, kitchen, basement) and contents. Number each box and add it to your list of boxes and their contents. This will make unloading easier.
- Finish packing personal items.
- Make a final inspection of the house to check for details which need to be taken care of before the next day.
- Plan a simple breakfast for the next morning which can be eaten without crockery.

## Moving day

- Strip the beds, but leave the bottom fitted sheets on mattresses and the bed assembled.
- Have the vacuum cleaner handy to clean behind the refrigerator and elsewhere, to leave the place in good condition for the new owner.
- Include your children in the day's activity. Let them see that all their treasures are being packed with the rest of the household belongings. The removal people will generally let

children visit the back of the van to see that, indeed, *everything* is going.

- As the removal people are finishing, make a final tour of the house to be sure you have everything. Don't forget the vacuum cleaner.
- Check, sign, and save a copy of the bill of lading. Be sure the address of your new home and the number of who is to be called if there are problems on the way are correct.
- Give the driver directions to the new address.
- Confirm delivery date and time.
- Leave keys with solicitor, estate agent, new occupant, or neighbour.
- Make sure all the windows and doors are closed and locked. Turn out all the lights.
- Check with the removal firm regarding final cost (determined on long-distance moves after van is weighed).

## Delivery day

- Be on hand to show the removal people where things go.
- Do not sign delivery papers until you've inspected for damage. If any loss or damage is noted, have the driver make specific notations of loss or damage on the papers you sign.
- If it's necessary to file a claim for damaged or missing items, notify the removal firm as soon as possible. They will send you claim forms.

## After arrival

- Find out about local transport such as bus or train schedules. Get appropriate maps.
- Research the emergency numbers you'll need in the new area. Get the location of the nearest hospital, and find out where the police and fire stations are.
- Enrol your children in school.
- Arrange for a friend or neighbour to keep an extra set of house and car keys.

- Locate local babysitters and check references.
- Check you are on the electoral register.
- Arrange for change of address on any other official papers.
- Register with a new doctor and dentist.

# 32: Hospital Stay

If you have advance warning that you'll be spending a night or two in the hospital, it's really no different from packing for a short trip. However long the hospital stay, the focus should be upon *comfort* and *practicality*. Below are some lists of things you should pack:

## Clothing

- Pyjamas/nightgown.
- Dressing gown.
- Slippers.
- Extra socks.
- Underwear − enough for the stay, plus a few extra pairs so you won't have to worry about getting laundry done.
- Clothing to wear home.

## Toiletries

- Brush and comb.
- Cosmetics.
- Creams/lotions.
- Dental floss.
- Deodorant.
- Hair accessories; travel-sized hair dryer.
- Hand mirror.
- Manicure items.
- Sanitary belt and pads/tampons if appropriate.
- Shampoo.
- Shaving kit.
- Showercap.

- Soap.
- Tissues.
- Toothbrush and toothpaste; mouthwash.

## Additional items

- Address book.
- Appointment book.
- Books or magazines.
- Clock (should be an inexpensive model).
- Spectacles.
- Memento — something soothing and personal. A touching letter or a photo of your children, family members, your pet, or your house.
- Money (small amount); change for telephone if you won't have a phone in the room.
- Pen or pencil; paper.
- Pillow, if the stay is to be a prolonged one and you'd feel more comfortable with your own.
- Plastic bags for laundry to be sent home.
- Playing cards or games.
- Radio with earphones.
- Vase (lightweight).

## Don't take

- Chequebook.
- Lots of money.
- Valuables or jewellery.

## For children

- Activities you can do with your child (cards, games, puppets) and those he or she can do alone (puzzles, colouring/activity books, picture or reading books, art projects using stickers).

- Book about the hospital experience, geared to the age of the child.
- Family photo.
- Favourite games.
- Nightlight.
- Special stuffed animal or blanket.

## *Find out in advance*

- Hospital rules and visiting hours.
- When family members can be with you other than during the usual visiting hours.
- How to get hold of the telephone; how you can be phoned.

## *While you're away from home*

- Contact someone and tell him or her where you are.
- Ask that person or a neighbour to pick up your post for you. If your stay is to be a long one, try to make arrangements for him or her to bring it to you.
- Cancel any appointments you had on the days you'll be in the hospital.
- Shut and lock windows.
- Unplug appliances.
- Adjust thermostat.
- Be sure the cooker is off.
- Take out the rubbish.
- Leave on a light.
- Lock all doors.

When I went to the hospital to have a baby, I probably had the only childbirth teacher who insisted that we did *not* pack in advance. She felt that we would have plenty of time to do that once we were in labour, and that with a first baby the longer we waited to enter the hospital, the better. Well, when I called my doctor to say I was in labour, he wanted me to come to the hospital immediately. I packed very quickly and somehow got there with everything I needed, so you *can* do it quickly if you must!

# 33: Job Search

There are two conditions under which people look for a new job: they want a change and have decided this is a good time to look for a better job or a new career; or they have been affected by industry redundancies, the closing of a division, management changes, and they've simply been let go.

Either way, the search requires the same effort; only the time frame is different. If the search is involuntary, time is of the essence, and a good job — not necessarily the perfect one — is the goal. If the search is voluntary, the person can afford to wait for a more ideal position.

It's often been said that getting a new job is a job in itself, which is why organisation is so important. If you're still working, you need a very organised method for pursuing leads and following up during the time you can spare for the job hunt. If you're currently unemployed, setting up a system for your job hunt will keep you from becoming depressed by treating it like the 9–5 job it should be.

## Organising your job search

- Buy a looseleaf notebook, dividers and paper, which will serve as the key to your entire job search. You will need to divide it into the following sections:

  ★ *Career goal.* This section is for recording your thoughts (and final decision) regarding what type of job you are currently looking for (or could do). Long-term career planning ideas should also be a part of this section.

  ★ *Contacts.* In this section, you will list *all* the people whom you should contact to help you with your search. Also note down names of helpful organisations and target companies (those which are likely to have the type of job you seek).

  ★ *Letters sent.* In this section, you will file copies of all the letters you send out. On the backs of the letters you can keep notes regarding subsequent conversations and meetings.

146

★*Interview preparations.* This section will include a list of general questions for which you will want to be prepared, as well as notes, brochures, annual reports, and other information regarding specific companies.

★*Follow up.* Keep a Thank You Note List and check off after you've written to someone; thank him or her for seeing you and re-emphasise any points you want to make. Once you have been interviewed at a company, letters and related material should be moved here. This will provide a comprehensive section to review when considering 'live' possibilities, as well as an organised method for following up.

● Order personalised stationery for covering letters. While it may seem like an extravagance if you're out of work, it will aid in the impression that you value yourself highly — remember that if you want people to value you enough to offer you a job, you need to value yourself. Also purchase some business-style notecards for thank yous as well as some stamps.

● Get an answering machine and record a pleasant, business-like message on it.

## Identifying your goal

● Be as specific as possible in setting a job goal. Use your notebook to record your thoughts. Take a long weekend or even a full week to consider exactly what type of job you're looking for (or could do). You may even want to visit a career counsellor for help in this area. Are you looking for exactly the same position you've had only in a different or larger environment? Or are you looking for a specific job in a field related to yours? Or are you seeking a career change?

● Now identify your target companies. You may already have a good number in mind, or your local library will have directories of firms in various industries. Ask the librarian for help.

● Consider salary expectations. This will probably involve some personal research. Find out what the going rate is in the field. If you're very experienced, you can probably ask for more. If you're a novice, you should expect less.

● Set goals regarding the number of letters to be sent and

contacts to be made each week. The number you establish
will depend on whether this is a full- or a part-time effort.

## *Preparing your c.v.*

● Tailor your c.v. to the type of job you are seeking. You may
need to write more than one. For example, a person with
writing or public relations experience in the health field
might prepare c.v.s for the following types of jobs:

★Public relations representative for a pharmaceutical
company  −  c.v. should emphasise PR background

★Editor of a health publication  −  c.v. should emphasise
editorial work experience

★Speechwriter for nonprofit health organisation  −  c.v.
should emphasise speechwriting experience

★Newspaper health reporter  −  c.v. should emphasise
writing and reporting experience

● Your c.v. should be no longer than one page. Remember, it's
the places where you've worked and your education which
get you the interview, so sacrifice other information.

● Describe your jobs with active verbs, emphasising
responsibilities and accomplishments: 'increased profits . . .'
'planned and executed project . . .' 'supervised staff of 30 . . .'

● Go over your c.v.'s layout and content with someone whose
business judgement you trust.

● Proof read your c.v. carefully. There's nothing worse than a
typographical error on one.

● Have your c.v. professionally printed and choose quality
paper.

● If you provide the names of references on your c.v., notify
them that they may be contacted.

## *Preparing your covering letter*

● Your covering letter is the gift wrapping for your c.v. It
should help make your c.v. stand out.

● Prepare a good basic letter (make a number of copies to use as
a starting point for each letter you write). This will ensure

against writer's block each time you send out your c.v. Keep in mind you will revise your letter each time, making it specific to the job and to the person to whom you are writing.

- Make the letter brief and to the point. Its content should focus on how you can help the company, not on how the company can help you.


## *Starting your search*

- Turn to the Contacts section of your notebook and begin to note down all the people who might help you find a job: family members, friends, business associates, acquaintances. Because 70 per cent of all jobs are found through personal contacts, such people are very important.
- Also note down executive recruitment agencies, careers advisers (such as your college careers adviser or even your employer, who may be offering help if many jobs are being phased out). Cut out newspaper and trade magazine job ads that sound interesting.
- Also keep up with trade journals and the business section of your newspaper. Cut out articles about people or companies which interest you. A person who is smart enough to follow up on an article may well get a job interview!
- You can also obtain new contacts by attending industry courses, meetings, lectures and seminars.
- Once you have a list of names, begin looking up addresses and telephone numbers. You may need to call for the person's exact title, the correct spelling of his or her name, and telephone extension.
- Be sure to list target companies where you would like to work. If you don't have an inside contact there, call and get the name of the person responsible for hiring in the division which interest you.
- Since your basic covering letter and c.v. are now prepared, you can immediately begin to approach the people you've listed on your Contacts page. In many cases, your goal is simply to be referred to someone who might have a job opening, so your covering letter should state that and note that you will follow up with a call.

- Photocopy each letter you send out, and file it in the Letters Sent section. Note in pencil the date the letter was actually posted as that will give you a better way of estimating when to follow up.

- Once the letters have been sent, use your diary to note the days on which you need to follow up.

- When you phone the person (as you must do with every letter you send out), keep notes regarding your conversation on the back of the covering letter. Note down the date of conversation and recommendations, and be sure to get the name of the secretary/assistant. That person is the key to your getting through again if you need to.

- Any recommendations you are given should be added to your Contacts list. Be sure to note by whom you were referred.

## *Prepare yourself before each interview*

- Research the company. If possible, talk to people who work there or who know others who do; try to locate and read any printed material about the company.

- Acquaint yourself with the company's product(s), if applicable.

- Think through the position for which you're applying, and note down any questions you'll want to ask. For example, you'll want to learn how the position works, what the responsibilities are, how much travel must be done, and where you would fit into the hierarchy. These questions should be filed in the Interview Preparations section of your notebook for handy reference.

- With the specific company and job in mind, consider any special questions the interviewer may ask.

- When considering the types of questions an interviewer will ask you, ask someone to help you rehearse. If you were eased out because of a company merger, you should have a positive explanation concerning what happened. If you've taken a couple of years off to go on a course, you ought to speak of the way that experience will benefit you in future jobs.

- Prepare an answer to the standard line: 'Tell me about yourself.' Don't be afraid to sell yourself! I once went to an interview where the opening statement was: 'Okay. You're on.'

• For artists, writers, and advertising and public relations executives, showing samples of work can be important on a job interview. If this applies to you, consider what samples you'll want to include and how you will package them. Also think in terms of creative selling. Plan the presentation you will make if you need to describe an advertising campaign, for example.

• Go through your wardrobe and choose two outfits you can wear to interviews (or shop for them, if necessary). That way one will be ready at all times. The outfits should look as expensive as the salary you aspire to make, and they should suit the style of the industry to which you're applying. For example, conservative attire is appropriate for an accounting firm, while a bit more flair is suitable in the advertising field.

• Choose outfits that make you feel comfortable. You don't want to be fussing with a stiff collar or a wraparound skirt that won't stay closed during the interview.

## The interview

• Be on time. Take a minute to make sure you're still looking neat before you enter the building.

• Choose a chair which places you comfortably near the interviewer.

• Try to assess how much time has been allotted for the interview. If the interviewer seems rushed, don't launch into any long stories. Pick up on his or her tempo.

• If you're not sure what the interviewer is looking for, try to encourage him or her to speak first. Respond accordingly, emphasising your skills and experience.

• Stick to the business at hand.

• Work at keeping good eye contact.

• Be positive about yourself and your attributes, and be enthusiastic about the job.

• Ask about their time schedule for choosing someone. As you leave, you should have a good idea of how much longer they expect to be interviewing for the position.

## *After the interview*

- As soon as you get home, make notes regarding the job, points discussed, and your impressions of the people and the company. This information should be filed in the Follow Up section of your notebook. On a separate sheet of paper (to be filed in the Interview Preparations section), note down any points of the conversation that went badly so you can review them before your next interview and thereby benefit from your mistakes.

- Promptly send any additional material the interviewer may have requested.

- Send a thank you note right away, emphasising any points you'd like the interviewer to remember (e.g. your experience at fundraising, your willingness to relocate).

- Do not wait to hear from the company. Based on the information you gained at the interview, choose an appropriate time to follow up, mark it in your diary, and call on that date to see what is happening.

- If you don't get through, don't be disheartened. Keep trying. Sometimes people are genuinely so busy they don't have time to return all their calls. Befriend the secretary/assistant, and perhaps he or she will tell you the best times to call.

- If you don't get a definite no, keep following up until the job is filled. If you do get a no, ask for advice. If you were a serious contender, the interviewer may well have some good suggestions and be pleased to help out.

It may never be a 'perfect' time to look for a job, but remember, you only need *one* job for the search to be a success! I've always believed that if you work steadily and persistently, you'll get what you want. Just keep trying!

# 34: Party Planning

A good number of years ago, I gave a party for my husband to celebrate an exciting career move he was making. Everything seemed to go wrong. The bartender came down with the flu the day of the event, the waitress I'd hired arrived inebriated, and the caterer didn't arrive until ten minutes before the guests were expected. When you're depending on other people, the unexpected is bound to happen. However, if you've done your homework, and as much as possible is organised, chances are everything will turn out fine. While things were a bit frenzied at the beginning of the evening, I knew it was successful when no one seemed to want to go home!

While we all know people who can pull a party together at the last minute and have it be a smash, for most of us planning a party requires foresight, thought, coordination, and a dash of good luck. To be able to have a gathering which both you *and* your guests can enjoy is an ideal celebration.

## General planning: six—eight weeks in advance

- Set a budget.
- Decide on what type of party you will have  —  cocktails, a sit-down dinner, Sunday lunch, an open house.
- Set the day, time, and place.
- Prepare a guest list (use your Household Notebook), and include on it guests' phone numbers in case you need to call them. After the invitations have been sent, keep the list and use it to keep track of RSVPs.
- If you're going to need a caterer, select the one you want to use and make certain they are free on that date.
- Buy invitations. You'll need additional time if ordering them.
- Using your Household Notebook, organise a timetable to keep track of tasks to be done ahead of time as well as on the day of the party. Add in personal details of your own as you think of them.

## *To do: three–four weeks in advance*

- Arrange for extra help if necessary. Will you need a bartender? Cook? Server? Babysitter?
- Arrange for entertainment, such as a pianist, if necessary.
- If the party will be held in cool weather, or if rain is a possibility, think about what you will do with the guests' coats. You may need to rent or borrow a coat rack.
- Consider your other needs. If you must rent/borrow chairs, dishes, glasses, serving pieces, or anything else, make the necessary arrangements.
- Think about what you want to wear. If you need to shop for something new, do so sufficiently in advance to allow time for any alterations. If you've chosen something you already own, make sure it is clean and in good repair.
- Order flowers. If ordering a floral centrepiece for a sit-down affair, be certain to specify a low one. You don't want the arrangement to block the vision of any of the guests at the dinner table.
- Address and post invitations.

## *Shopping: three–four weeks in advance*

- Plan your menu. Whether you're serving dinner for eight or just hors d'oeuvres, write down each dish you plan to have. If working with a caterer, consult with him or her.
- If you're doing the party on your own, try to select some dishes you can cook ahead and freeze.
- Assemble all the recipes for the dishes which need to be prepared.
- Go through the recipes and make a complete list of all ingredients. Even make a note of the items you're 'sure' you have. There's nothing worse than discovering you're out of a necessary ingredient on the day of the party!
- Check the list against the items you have on hand.
- Divide the list into categories for easier shopping, or simply transfer the needed items on to one of the form grocery lists described in Chapter 26.

- Go back through the recipes and separate out those dishes which can be made in advance. Also group together the recipes which will need to be made at the last minute. (Although I don't recommend last-minute dishes!)

- Consider your drink needs. A well-stocked bar would contain a good representation of the following:

  ★Beer                               ★Rum
  ★Brandy                             ★Vermouth
  ★Champagne                          ★Vodka
    (for a special celebration)       ★Whisky
  ★Gin                                ★Wine, red and white

- Ask at the off-licence or wine merchant about how much you should get based on the number of guests who are coming. Check you can hire glasses if you will need more than you possess.

- You'll also want to have on hand:

  ★Cola and diet soda                 ★Mineral water
  ★Ginger ale                         ★Olives
  ★Juice, tomato and orange           ★Soda water
  ★Lemons                             ★Tonic water
  ★Limes

If you know the drinking habits of your friends, you may be able to narrow this list somewhat.

- Here are some miscellaneous items you may need to shop for:

  ★Candles                            ★Plastic glasses
  ★Paper plates/napkins/              ★Decorations
    cups (if not using china)         ★Placecards

- In addition, you will want to have the following on hand:

  ★Bottle opener                      ★Ice bucket
  ★Coasters                           ★Matches for candles
  ★Corkscrew                          ★Napkins
  ★Dish cloths (have extras on        ★Paper towels
    hand)                             ★Placemats
  ★Guest towels                       ★Records or tapes as
  ★Hand soaps                           background music
  ★Hangers                            ★Tablecloth
  ★Ice (buy or make in advance
    and freeze)

- If shopping will be done by two people, decide now who will purchase what.

## To do: one week in advance

- Call to confirm all orders and arrangements, including any help you have coming (bartender, cook, server, babysitter, musician), and tell them to arrive earlier than they are really needed. That way traffic problems or some type of delay won't cause you to panic. They should still arrive well before the guests do.
- Make sure you have plenty of ashtrays on hand.
- Be sure you have enough hangers.

## Cooking: one week in advance

- Prepare and freeze any of the dishes which can be made in advance.

## Cooking: one – two days in advance

- Organise the dishes which need to be made the day of the party – especially those (such as stir frying) which have to be done just prior to or at the time of the meal. Pre-measure as many ingredients as you can and keep them in small dishes or measuring cups, covered and wrapped in plastic wrap. Group them by recipe in your refrigerator.

## To do: one – two days in advance

- Get out the various serving pieces and linen you will need for the party.
- Get down the china and crystal, and check to see if they need to be washed.
- Get out the silver if you are using any and see if it needs polishing.
- Clean your home.

- Think about your space needs for the event. Should the furniture be arranged differently?
- Be sure you have a good supply of dish cloths and paper towels on hand.
- Arrange to have cash to pay the help.
- Create a time chart to help guide you on the day of the party. Plan at what time you need to set the table (early), when the oven needs to be turned on, and so on. This type of chart is also helpful for anyone who is going to help you. Create a list of their tasks and the time at which each should be done so that everything will go like clockwork.

## To do: the day of the event

- Set the table as early as possible.
- If your building has a doorman, give the guest list to him.
- Clear off the kitchen counters.
- Run the dishwasher before the guests come so that it is empty and ready for party dishes.
- Do a last-minute straightening of the house, and wipe down the bathrooms to clean off waterspots and fingerprints.
- Put out hand towels.
- Put out ashtrays.

## Food preparation: the day of the event

- Get out any of the utensils and dishes you will need for cooking.
- Use a tray to organise the ingredients needed to prepare dishes that must be made just prior to or during the party.
- Use the kitchen timer as a reminder for various things, such as to start preparing a certain dish or to take something out of the refrigerator.
- Cheese should be removed from the refrigerator one hour before so that it will reach room temperature before being served.
- Red wine should be opened an hour in advance so that it can

'breathe'. White wine should be chilled in advance, and can even be opened and recorked before refrigerating to save you time once your guests arrive.

● Prepare breadbaskets in advance.

● Fill ice bucket.

## For the future

● Keep a record in the back of your Household Notebook (see 'Household — General'), or create an 'Entertaining' category in your filing cabinet, which should include a guest list of those who attended as well as those who were unable to come. Note the date, time, and food served, and keep an itemised list of costs. Make notes regarding things that could have gone better, comments on the food, and ideas for the future. This will be helpful in planning another party.

# 35: Travel Planning

For some people, travel problems begin the moment a trip is being planned – so many unfamiliar things to do, so many details to take care of . . . What flights will be best? Where shall we stay? What arrangements must be worked out at home? The questions go on and on.

For others, problems don't arise until it's almost time for them to leave. They didn't get as much office work done as they'd intended; they're worried about leaving the children behind; they're exhausted from burning the midnight oil by packing at the last minute; and there's always the nagging feeling that something has been forgotten . . .

Yet whether you're travelling for business or pleasure, being away provides you with a change of scene that can be interesting, fun, and often relaxing. An unsettling departure detracts from some of these benefits since the disorganised traveller must often contend with more than his or her share of unforeseen problems. The following travellers would have benefited from better planning:

One family neglected to book their airline seats at the time they bought their tickets. They arrived at the airport to discover that the only seats available for the parents and two toddlers were four separate seats in different parts of the plane. Only after several discussions with airline personnel were they able to get their seats changed.

Another woman grew up in a family where they often went on long car trips. Invariably, their first stop was pulling into a petrol station so that they could phone a neighbour (who had a house key) to go in and make sure the morning kettle had been turned off.

Travelling *is* hard work in terms of detail management, and of course, the above examples are very human stories. However, think how much more pleasant your trip would be if you had a useful checklist (for such things as turning off the kettle), and had thought through your trip plans and made certain standing arrangements in order to minimise the disruptions of travel.

Here are some suggestions which should improve your frame of mind at departure, make your time away more enjoyable, and help better prepare you for a smooth return.

## *Advance planning*

- Use a good travel agent, one whose knowledge of plane routes and air fares can save you both time and money. Make sure your agent knows your seating preference (smoking or non-smoking, aisle or window), so that he or she can book a seat and get your boarding pass for you ahead of time.

- You can often arrange in advance for a special meal on the plane. Most airlines offer low-calorie, low- or no-salt, low-cholesterol, vegetarian, kosher, fish, and children's meals. You should let your travel agent know about these special needs.

- If you're travelling abroad, purchase enough of the appropriate currency before you leave to pay for getting to your hotel, making phone calls, and the like.

- Also for foreign travel, make a photocopy of your passport. If the original is lost or stolen, the nearest embassy can use the photocopy to issue a new one.

- Make an itinerary of your trip. Include phone numbers and addresses of the places you'll be staying each night as well as airline and flight details. Give one copy to someone at work; another copy to the person looking after your home, and take one with you. Pack another copy in your suitcase, so that if your luggage gets lost, it can be sent to you at any stage of your trip.

- At the office, delegate as much as possible. Leave clear instructions as to how certain issues should be handled so that you won't have to do it when you return.

- Look through your diary. Reschedule any appointments which fall during the time you'll be away.

- Plan for a free day when you return. If you're going on a trip of any length, try to schedule it so that you can stay at home on your first day back. This will give you the time to take care of the laundry and cleaning and pick up the dog, etc.

- Does someone need to take care of your plants or pet? Leave him or her written instructions as to what to do. You can streamline this process by writing the instructions once. Then make photocopies of the information and file it for future trips. That way you'll never need to write those instructions again.

- If you have household help, tell them you'll be away and discuss any special tasks to be undertaken. If there is no ironing because you are gone, would you like to have the cupboards cleaned instead?

- If no one will be at home while you're gone, go through the refrigerator to throw out groceries that will spoil. Stock up on items you can freeze and use after your return.

- Pack (see Chapter 36). Start this two days prior to departure.

- Confirm your plane reservation and double-check your overnight arrangements.

- Take any phone numbers or travel directions you may need.

- As a welcome home gift, put fresh linen on the bed for your return.


## *For the children*

If children will be staying behind with a relative or friend, here are a few additional suggestions:

- Post a copy of your itinerary in a location where it can be seen by child-minder and children alike. Even a three- or four-year-old may take comfort in having the itinerary read to him or her.

- Make emergency and general household phone numbers easily accessible, and be sure everyone, including children, know where they are. Be sure to leave a telephone number of someone to call for back-up help.

- Assemble a While We're Away notebook – invaluable for those looking after children as well as teenagers who are old enough to stay alone. Note exactly what should be done 'if the dog gets sick . . .' or 'if the power goes out . . .' or 'if the basement floods . . .' or 'if the washing machines goes on the blink . . .' What's more, once the notebook has been prepared, it need only be updated for future trips.

● Arrange dates (and time of day) when you will phone.

## *Before you leave*

● Check to see you have keys, directions, money, tickets, and itinerary.
● If you live alone or if other family members will be away too, you'll also want to do the following:
  ★Run the dishwasher early so that it will have finished before you depart.
  ★Shut and lock windows.
  ★Unplug appliances.
  ★Adjust thermostat.
  ★Be sure the cooker is off.
  ★Take out the rubbish.
  ★Leave on a light and/or radio with a timer.
  ★Lock all doors.

## *The trip*

● Travel in comfortable clothes such as no-crease knit or wool jersey slacks. Wear a sweater (in the summer you can wear a light cotton one) in case it's chilly in the cabin, ferry or car.
● If you are travelling from cold to warmer weather, consider wearing layered clothing. Upon reaching your destination, you can remove the outer layers and you'll be all set for the new climate!
● Get a copy of a current pocket flight guide. If your plane is cancelled or you miss a flight, you can map out a new flight plan for yourself.
● Carry change for pay telephones.
● If this is a business trip, take along a special file or envelope to keep track of the information and papers you will be collecting (business cards, reports, fliers, receipts, and so on). If your work is going to generate a lot of paperwork, try to handle as much as possible while you're away.
● Plan to arrive at the airport or ferryport one hour early to check in and check your bags before departure.

## *At the hotel*

- When you are first shown to your hotel room, check the bathroom, bed, and pillows. Test the air-conditioner or heater and try out the television. If you're not satisfied, now is the time to discuss the possibility of a room change.

- Once in a satisfactory room, check for the fire exit. Read the hotel literature regarding escape methods.

- Request a hair drier, ironing board, or iron, if needed. Most hotels can supply these at little or no charge.

- If you'll be in a rush the next morning, place your breakfast order with room service the night before.

## *Your return*

While it always feels good to come home, the part that is often the least pleasant is coping with the accumulation of post and messages which have come in while you were away. Here are some tips to help you manage better:

- If you've been away for a long period of time, you probably have cleared your diary for the first day back so that you have a day to take care of chores around home.

- Both at home and at the office, set aside at least one hour to sort through post and paperwork. Try to do this as soon as possible after your arrival.

- Set priorities on the items you will handle first.

- Try to return all telephone calls at one sitting.

- At the office, check with colleagues about any events which may have occurred while you were away.

- Check your diary so that you're prepared for forthcoming events.

- Select reading material or simple work projects which you might be able to fit into odd moments of the day, such as while you're waiting at the bank. Carry those items with you and pull them out when you have time.

# 36: Travel Packing

What happened to my best friend should never happen to anyone. When her husband was asked to argue a case in front of a major court, she wanted to go along. Upon arriving at the hotel, she opened her suitcases and realised that in her excitement she had packed all the right blouses and jackets but had totally forgotten to pack her skirts. She literally had nothing to wear!

Had my friend been using an orderly system for packing, she would have arrived with all her outfits intact. However, many people are nearly paralysed by the decision-making process involved in taking a trip, so they tend to prepare in a haphazard manner – usually at the last minute. (My sister's honeymoon was delayed because instead of going directly to the airport after the reception, they had to go back to her new husband's flat so he could pack!)

One client of mine starts early enough; however, to me, her system seems equally fraught with potential disasters. She calls her method the 'lazy woman's' way of packing. About a week before her trip she opens her suitcase and just keeps throwing into it things she knows she'll want. In addition to the inconvenience of having certain items out of circulation for a week, this approach offers no method for verifying that she has what she needs. Apparently it works for her, but there *are* better ways to pack.

Developing a system that works for you will make packing a simple procedure, which will allow you to leave on any kind of trip, be it for business or pleasure, feeling comfortable and well prepared.

Let's begin by checking to be sure you have the right travel equipment:

- Check your luggage to make sure it is roomy and sturdy enough to accommodate what you plan to take. If you're buying new items, look for lightweight bags. Larger pieces should have wheels built into the bottom to make them easier to transport.

- Invest in a good piece of light, hand luggage so that for short

164

trips you don't need to put your bag into the hold. Luggage still mysteriously goes to other destinations, and although the airlines almost invariably track it down, the first few days of a trip can be ruined if it's missing.

• Be sure you have luggage tags for your bags. Some airlines insist that all suitcases have external labels, so you'll save yourself time at the airport if your bags are already tagged.

• Visit a shop that carries travellers' aids such as small alarm clocks, showercaps, portable washing lines, collapsible plastic hangers, sewing kits, travel irons, electric voltage adaptors, and small plastic bottles. But don't buy anything you won't really use.

## Planning

Planning is the next step, and several weeks before (when possible) is not too early to begin thinking about what you'll need for the trip. You may need extra time to get shoes repaired or to shop for items you don't already have (bathing suit, etc.).

As soon as you know you are going out of town, begin to prepare a checklist of everything you think you'll need for your trip. You can probably use the checklist below as a starting point.

## Travel checklist

### Clothing

| | | |
|---|---|---|
| ___ Belts | ___ Hats | ___ Slippers |
| ___ Blouses | ___ Jackets | ___ Slips |
| ___ Boots | ___ Jeans | ___ Socks |
| ___ Bras | ___ Nightie/nightshirt | ___ Stockings |
| ___ Coat | ___ Raincoat | ___ Suits |
| ___ Dresses | or anorak | ___ Sweaters |
| ___ Dressing gown | ___ Scarves | ___ Swimsuit |
| ___ Evening clothes | ___ Shirts | ___ Ties |
| ___ Gloves | ___ Shoes | ___ Trousers |
| ___ Handkerchiefs | ___ Skirts | ___ Underwear |

## Grooming items

___ Aftershave
___ Brush and comb
___ Creams/lotions
___ Cottonballs
___ Cottonswabs
___ Dental floss
___ Deodorant
___ Eye makeup
   ___ Liner
   ___ Mascara
   ___ Pencil
   ___ Shadow and brush
___ Feminine needs
___ Hairclips, pins,
or ornaments
___ Hair dryer
___ Hair curlers
or curling iron
___ Hair spray
___ Lipstick and lip pencil
___ Make-up

___ Blusher and brush
___ Concealer
___ Foundation
___ Powder
___ Manicure items
___ Moistened towelettes
___ Mouthwash
___ Nailbrush
___ Perfume
___ Powder (body)
___ Razor blades or
electric razor
___ Shampoo, rinse, and/or
conditioner
___ Shaving kit
___ Showercap
___ Soap
___ Sunblock lotion/Suntan oil
___ Talc
___ Toothbrush and toothpaste
___ Tweezers

## Medical

___ Adhesive bandages
___ Back-up pair of glasses or
prescription for glasses (Very
important! Ideally, leave an old pair
permanently packed.)
___ First-aid ointment

___ Insect repellent
___ Prescription and necessary
nonprescription medications
___ Thermometer
___ Vitamins

## Additional items

___ Address book
___ Alarm clock
___ Camera and film
___ Cash/traveller's cheques
___ Cheque book
___ Converter, electric, for foreign
travel
___ Credit cards
___ Cufflinks and collar stays
___ Jewellery
___ Passport/visa for foreign travel
___ Pen

___ Playing cards
___ Radio
___ Reading material
___ Safety pins
___ Scissors
___ Sewing kit
___ Stamps
___ Sunglasses
___ Torch
___ Travel tickets
___ Umbrella (collapsible)

• Using the checklist, consider every aspect of your trip and note down clothing, accessories, medications, reading material, and emergency supplies. Try to anticipate everything you might need for the locale you'll be in and the kinds of things you'll be doing.

● When planning what clothes to take, prepare for all weather possibilities. When Indian summer turns to crisp autumn overnight, you could be left shivering if you didn't pack a sweater or jacket of some kind. But be realistic. Overdoing 'just-in-case' items can weigh you down.

● If you're reluctant to leave one or two 'just-in-case' items behind, try to determine whether or not you *could* buy it at your destination if you needed to. A friend felt it was worth travelling with a one-week supply of disposable nappies for her one-year-old when she learned that they were not yet available where she was visiting overseas. To help you make such decisions, talk to people who have recently visited the places you are going.

● Avoid excess bulk. Select clothes that coordinate, and keep your choices to a minimum. Most of us take too much.

● Buy a small folding coat rack where you can display all items of clothing before you pack them. Seeing your clothes together often helps you eliminate the excess or discover a problem (missing button, stain on shirt, etc.). Many clients have reported night-before-departure panic when they realise that a favourite suit needed cleaning and there was no time to get it done. It's important to pack your clothes in first-class condition − clean, uncreased, and ready to wear.

## *The 'ever-ready' toilet kit*

When it comes to packing, a permanently prepared toilet kit is a must. Why pack and repack the same items every trip?

● For the kit, choose a small case (preferably a transparent, soft-sided, waterproof bag). The number of toiletries to be packed should be the determining factor as to bag size.

● Invest in an extra toothbrush, shaver, and hairbrush to keep permanently packed in your kit.

● Buy travel-sized toothpaste, shampoo, lotion and aspirin, reserved for travel use.

● Transfer items such as your facial cleanser into small plastic bottles (available at chemists). Any liquids you feel you must take should be in tightly sealed plastic containers, filled only three quarters of the way and put in secured plastic bags. At the end of each trip, refill any that are getting low.

- Compartmentalise your toilet bag for easy use. Divide essentials into categories: body care (lotion, deodorant), make-up (foundation, lipstick), hair care (shampoo, conditioner) and dental items (toothpaste, toothbrush and floss).

- Try to travel with as few spillables as possible. But if you feel you absolutely must take your own bottle of kaolin and morphine, wrap and pack it *very* carefully, preferably in your toilet bag. My cousin learned that lesson the hard way when he opened his suitcase and discovered his bottle of kaolin coating everything but his stomach. To ensure against this, carry doubtful items on the plane with you.

- Use scented lotion instead of perfume. It saves space and avoids the chance of costly spills.

## Your hand luggage

Items that are too important to be without and items that will make plane travel more pleasant are those you'll pack in your hand luggage.

- Buy a lightweight, compartmentalised bag (smaller than the bag you would use for clothes for a short trip).

- Plan to carry tickets, jewellery, toiletries, important papers, maps, money, your address book, passport (for foreign travel) and reading matter.

- For additional comfort: Pressurisation on planes dries out the air, so a small tube of moisturiser or hand lotion can keep you feeling refreshed. Men might carry a disposable razor for a quick shave before reaching their destination. Other items to consider carrying on board might include toothbrush and paste, tissues, a small container of freshening facial cleanser, and a pen and pocket-sized notebook for jotting down thoughts, questions and ideas.

# Packing

You should actually begin putting items in your bags about two days before your departure. It's too tiring to pack the night before when you'll have other details to take care of such as last-minute instructions to colleagues or to the person who will be watching the house, and so on. (I shudder when I think of one friend who is always up until 3am the night before her trip doing laundry and ironing . . .)

• Begin by hanging or laying out your garments.

• When departing with more than one piece of luggage, divide your clothes among the suitcases. This avoids being left with only a suitcase full of your shoes and underwear if your bag filled with suits and dresses is lost.

• Just as shops often use tissue paper to transport your purchases crease-free, you can do the same by saving the paper acquired in gifts and purchases to fold within your clothing when packing. Some people like to roll their clothing rather than laying it flat. With some items it takes up less room and can prevent creasing.

• Put heavier, most crease-resistant items (sweaters, dressing gown, jeans) on the bottom. To minimise wasted space, alternate the layers of remaining clothes: first, a layer from left to right, then one from front to back.

• Store underwear and tights/stockings in separate, transparent plastic bags.

• Pack items inside one another. For example, socks and shoehorn should go inside shoes, hosiery inside a folded sweater.

• Put your shoes, paired, in plastic bags or cloth shoebags and place them along the sides of the suitcase as you are packing. Since these will probably be the heaviest items in your luggage, keep them to a minimum.

• The nooks and crannies that remain should be filled with rolled-up belts, scarves, ties and underwear. These items will cushion and hold the other items when the suitcase is closed and standing upright.

• If you can anticipate your needs ahead of time, make sure that the last layer of clothing you pack will be the articles you will need first upon your arrival.

- Plastic bags are useful for laundry and to hold clothes that may be damp.
- Some people like to pack clothing still on hangers. Women may want to take along skirt hangers since few hotels can be counted on to have them.
- Pack a lightweight carrier bag. It is bound to be useful while you are away and you can use it coming home if you need to.
- Add a sachet to keep your clothes smelling fresh.
- When packing to come home, you may fear you'll never be able to fit in the extras you bought. Roll your clothes instead of laying them flat.
- Keep your checklist! While there will always be variations in clothing, it will serve as a helpful guide in packing the next time. You need never forget your address book, sunglasses, or belt again!

# Section 6
## ~
# Personal Agenda

# 37: Beauty Routine

I once needed to attend a meeting with a beauty/fashion consultant and since we both lived in the same area, we decided to share a taxi. I was very surprised when she came downstairs and got into the taxi fully dressed but with no make-up. She then proceeded to pull out a small pouch and spend 10 of the 15 minutes we were in the cab applying foundation, eye make-up, blusher and lipstick. When we arrived, she looked terrific!

Since most of us can't count on having a hands-free taxi ride for doing our make-up (let alone having the ability to apply make-up on a bump-filled excursion), it's important to establish a simple beauty regimen which becomes an easy and natural part of the day.

The key to an efficient beauty routine lies partly in organising your supplies so they are accessible and convenient, but it also has to do with making the routine a matter of habit.

Here's how to get started.

## Simplifying your morning routine

- Consider your haircut. With today's easy styles, there is no reason to wear one which requires much effort. Choose a cut that is easy to care for, and then get it trimmed regularly so that you benefit fully from the easy styling.

- Consider your skin care system. Are you mixing and matching various soaps and moisturisers depending on what's handy that day? Instead, choose one basic skin care treatment, perhaps one where all the products are designed to go together. It will be easier to follow, and you'll have two or three products to store instead of many.

- Consider your make-up routine. Try to establish one or two simple 'looks', using minimal amounts of products. Visit a make-up consultant at one of your local department stores to help you select complementary products and make a fresh start.

## *Organising your make-up*

- Evaluate the area where you put on your make-up. Is this the best place to do it? Is the lighting good? Is there a convenient spot for storing your make-up? If you use a dressing-table, devote a drawer to it. If you apply your make-up in the bathroom, devote part of the bathroom cabinet to it.

- Go through your make-up and throw out what you no longer use. Also throw out those items that are more than a year old or that you think you might not use again – you probably won't, and make-up doesn't age well. Some products gather bacteria and can even be dangerous to use if allowed to sit for a long period of time.

- Buy a compartmentalised plastic container for your make-up with separate slots for lipstick and brushes, and spots for foundation and blusher.

- Within the container, organise the items by type. For example, store together all brushes in one spot, all lipsticks in another, and all eye shadows in another. Items used first (or most frequently) should be most accessible.

- Consider an all-purpose make-up kit (available at most department stores), complete with coordinated eye, cheek, and lip colours.

- When your make-up needs to be altered with the changing of the seasons (more moisturising products for winter; lighter products for summer) pack away the cosmetics you don't use during the current season.

- When you find a product that works, stick with it.

- Keep lotion and handcream in all the rooms where you use it – in the bathroom, the kitchen, and the bedroom. A pump-style lotion dispenser saves times, and for double duty, rub cream or lotion into your cuticles while you're applying it to your hands.

- Use clear nail polish. It's easier to touch up if it gets chipped, and it doesn't need to be applied as frequently as coloured polish.

- Pick up travel-sized make-up items and extras of lipstick, mascara and blusher to store in a make-up pouch at the office or to carry with you in your handbag.

- For travel, keep a lightweight make-up bag stocked and ready to go with all your essentials. Stock up on travel-sized quantities of skin care and make-up items, and buy sample sizes of items such as lotion and shampoo. When you get home, replace your travel supplies so you'll automatically be ready for the next trip.

## Establishing your routine

Next time you take a trip, note how much more you must concentrate on applying your make-up simply because your products aren't where your hands are trained to find them. If you've not yet developed a system which your hands seem to perform automatically, you've not simplified your routine as much as possible. Here's how to do so:

- Choose a specific time of day (after your morning shower or before breakfast) when you apply your make-up, and do it at that same time every day – including weekends. The more automatically the routine is performed, the more quickly you can do it; and the more assured you can be that the doorbell won't ring when you still don't have on your make-up.

- Establish a set routine for putting on your make-up (concealer followed by foundation, followed by powder, etc.).

- In the morning, stay in one room until you've finished everything you need to do there. For example, after your shower, stay in the bathroom and do your make-up while you're waiting for your hair to dry.

- Establish a set time for weekly manicures and pedicures so they become an expected part of your schedule.

- 'Double up' on time. Time spent commuting can be perfect for tummy-firming exercises. If you're not driving, you can also touch up your make-up. Time spent watching the news or your favourite television programme is a perfect opportunity to give yourself a manicure. And before sitting down at your desk, give yourself a facial which can work while you pay your bills.

# 38: Dates to Remember

If you've cornered the market on belated birthday cards (or even if you've only missed one or two special dates this year), you're causing yourself needless frustration by having forgotten to send good wishes to someone you care about.

When it comes to special occasions, late is better than never, but nothing beats being on time. All that's required for remembering important dates is a simple system that works for you. Here are several from which to choose.

## The birthday book

Stationery and gift shops usually carry these special date-books (actually called birthday books) which are designed for keeping track of special occasions. Museum giftshops frequently sell ones that are especially beautiful. One advantage of the birthday book is that is can be used year after year, so you need to record only once the dates you want to remember.

- Buy a birthday book you find appealing. (You may want to buy two or three – they make great gifts!)
- Enter all the special occasions of which you want to be reminded.
- As you make each entry, also note the year of the birth or, for anniversaries, the year of the marriage. That way you can always work out how old Mary's son is, and fortieth birthdays and silver wedding anniversaries won't slip by without appropriate fanfare!
- Consult your birthday book at the end of each month to note the special dates for the weeks ahead.
- The only way the birthday book can fail you is if you forget to use it. If you're just starting out with this system, make a note in your diary or Tickler File (see opposite) for the next few months to remind yourself to consult it.

## Diary reminders

If you don't think you can adjust to referring to a special book regularly, a diary reminder method whereby you note a person's birthday or a special occasion on the upcoming year's diary may work better for you.

● Go through your diary today and note all the special occasions you intend to remember.

● Use a special colour of ink, perhaps red or turquoise, to distinguish these notations from other information.

● In late December, sit down and transfer all the dates from the old diary into the new one. Because you've used a special colour, the notations should pop out at you, thus minimising the chance of error when making the annual date transfer.

## Tickler files

Your Tickler Files (see Chapter 10) offer another simple way to be reminded of special occasions. With this system, you'll pull out your reminder at the beginning of each month.

● Using a separate card for each month, record special occasions on index cards which can then be filed in the appropriate file folders.

● In order to plan and buy in advance, put the February card in the January file (so that in January you'll be thinking of the February dates you need to shop for) and the March card in the February file, and so on. This gives you enough warning to plan for occasions falling early in the following month.

## Following through

Regardless of the system you choose, nothing works unless you follow through.

● Establish a regular time each month to review coming dates and to shop for all the cards or gifts you are going to need in the coming weeks.

● Purchase a selection of blank cards that will serve a variety of purposes (get well, congratulations, thank you, happy birthday) for those times when something unexpected comes up.

By choosing and using one of these systems, you can say good-bye to those last-minute dashes to the shops to get a card or gift. (For tips on gift shopping for holidays and special occasions, see Chapter 40.)

What's more, you may gain quite a reputation. One well-organised friend tells a story of the time her in-laws became quite distressed when they didn't receive an anniversary card from her. 'They were sure something dreadful was going on if I forgot to send a card,' Gail explains. 'Of course when they called, we were fine, and we were all reminded that everyone's human. However, I must tell you, I haven't forgotten them since!'

# 39: Errands

How many times have you arrived home from doing errands, only to remember that there was something you forgot? As you venture back out, it may seem like the errands are running you rather than the other way around!

One day I dropped into my neighbour's to see if she needed any help with arrangements for a party she was having that night. She commented about how tired she was from going to the shops. Well, it turned out she wasn't tired from *one* trip to the shops; she was tired from three. Each time she had come back home, she remembered something else she needed and had to go back out again!

With a little creative planning you can avoid these last-minute dashes and streamline the chores that fill your free time.

## Establishing a system

- An ongoing list is the first step in getting errands done more efficiently. I recommend using your looseleaf Household Notebook (see Chapter 22). Establish a section for items 'To Buy' (chandelier lightbulbs, gloves, a new couch), 'To Fix' (the dress that needs to go to the seamstress or the doll that needs to be taken in for repair), and 'To Do' (donate blood, go to the library, check new hotel for possible place for Mum and Dad to stay). Then you can transfer the items you plan to do each day on to your 'To Do' list in your diary. Or if you plan a full day of errands, simply take the notebook with you.
- Teach family members to tell you about general errands (shoes that need re-heeling, shirts for the laundry, the blender isn't working, etc.) which must be entered into your notebook. Regarding items to be purchased (such as shaving cream, shampoo, adhesive tape), tell the family to let you know when the supply is *low*, not out.
- Anticipate forthcoming needs. Buy a season's supply of

178

hosiery, several sheets of stamps, and five or six tubes of toothpaste (especially if you catch a sale!) at the same time.

● Establish a table, desk, or chair near the front door where you can lay out all you need for the next round of errands (suits for the cleaners; an item to be returned to the shop). Your keys, handbag, and briefcase should also be located here for an easy exit.

## Consolidating your errands

● Always plan your errands around your schedule, not the other way around!

● On Sunday evening, sit down with your Household Notebook and your diary, which should also have space for each day's 'To Do' list. Are any of your upcoming appointments in an area where you can accomplish another chore? If so, write a reminder in your diary for that day.

● For regular errands to be done during the week, select one or two blocks of time (after work on Tuesday? during lunch time on Thursday?) when you can conveniently get some errands done. Then list in your diary what you plan to accomplish.

● Organise your errands by location. For example, before going out to do errands around your area, map out a route so that each stop takes you part of the way to the next one. Once you're finished, you can go directly on to your next activity or plan a circular route which brings you back home again.

● Plan to do all your banking for the week at one time. Try to shop or bank during periods of least activity – mid-morning rather than noon, for example. Get into the habit of filling out transaction forms in advance.

## Carry-all convenience

● Buy an unstructured nylon bag to use for errands. These carry-alls are light, completely collapsible, and easy to wipe out in case of spills. Many feature long straps for shoulder-carrying.

- Also buy a waterproof that folds into a small pouch. The waterproof is of lighter weight and more compact than an umbrella when not in use, and when needed, it frees your umbrella hand. Also tuck into your carry-all an extra plastic shopping bag or two to cover or to carry extra packages in a shower.

## The homecoming

'*What* do you do when you get home with all the packages?' asked one of my clients who told a story about how she had been putting things away for half an hour one night when she realised she hadn't even taken off her coat.

Other people tend to arrive home, dump their packages, and let days go by before putting everything away.

Remember the chair or table near the door? Well, that's your home base for arrival too. Here's how to proceed from there:

- Unload all parcels there.
- As soon as you've put away your coat and hat, return and start putting things away.
- Begin by putting away perishables.
- Categorise items by room to avoid unnecessary trips to each room.

## Tips to save wear and tear

- Take advantage of any merchant who will pick up and deliver. (If your dry cleaner is one of them, keep a checklist of items left there in your Household Notebook to verify that all is returned.)
- Any time you can find a professional − manicurist, haircutter, exercise instructor − who will come to your home or office, take advantage of it.
- If you have extra time before or after an appointment, pull out your Notebook and see what you can get done.
- 'Do it when you pass it.' If you happen to pass by a specialist shop and remember something you need, go in and buy it right away.
- Ask family members to help out with errands.

## *What to do when you dread doing an errand*

We all have certain things we just hate doing, like returning an item or dropping things off at a tailor who is on the other side of town. Here's how to overcome your own resistance:

● Ask, 'What will happen if I don't do this task?' If there are no dire consequences, forget it.

● Cooperate. Team up with another parent for getting the kids back and forth to their dance class, for example.

● Swap. If your neighbour will shop for something you need near her office, offer to do something special for her.

● Nervous about returning goods? Enlist a friend for moral support.

● Pay someone to do it for you. It might be worth it!

# 40: Gift Shopping

How often have you received one of the following as a gift:

- A shirt or blouse two sizes too big — or too small?
- A sweater in a shade you detest and would *never* wear?
- An outfit that would have been perfect for you — five years ago?
- An absolutely useless object?

While there is no way to prevent others from giving you the unwanted and the unusable, you can avoid contributing to the white elephant collections of others by organising your gift-buying system.

By making gift-buying a year-round process you will save time (no rushing around at the last minute) and money (how often have you said, 'I don't care what it costs, I need a gift for tonight!'). You'll also find that your gifts are more appreciated because they'll show the thought and planning that went into them.

Buying gifts for others is a two-step process. First, you need to *remember* that a birthday or anniversary is drawing near (see Chapter 38); then you need to have a system for choosing an appropriate gift.

## Establishing a system

- Establish a Gifts file in your filing cabinet (as suggested in Chapter 10) where you can store gift lists as well as clippings and articles about perfect gifts for family and friends.
- Buy index cards.
- On the front of each card, write the name of a friend, family member, or business associate with whom you exchange gifts. Note the date of birth (and other important occasions). Make notes about the person's likes and dislikes. Note sizes, favourite colours, hobbies, and special interests. The front of the card will also be used for noting gift ideas. Whenever you

think of a terrific gift idea, write it down immediately! The front of a card for a friend might look like this:

---

TRACY ROLANDS

Birthday: March 11, 1950

Favourite colours: pink and blue
Blouse size: 12
Sweater: medium
Collects antique clothing and loves floppy hats
Hobbies include photography and home restoration
Gift ideas: handmade photo albums (at J.J. and Co.); also try
country auction for other ideas

---

- On the back of the card, keep a running record of what you give each year. That way you'll avoid giving the same gift twice. A sample card for your father might look like this:

---

DAD

| | |
|---|---|
| Birthday 1985 | book on coin collecting |
| Christmas 1985 | shirt and tie |
| Birthday 1986 | engraved shoe horn |
| Christmas 1986 | V-neck sweater |

---

- How to use the system? At the beginning of each month, when you consult your birthday book or Tickler File (see Chapter 38) and note down whose birthday is coming up, simply go to your Gifts file and take out the appropriate index cards. You've automatically got all the information you need to buy a thoughtful, personal gift!

## *Getting it done*

- See Chapter 39 for tips on faster, easier shopping.
- Scout out small boutiques and specialist shops where you can buy unusual items without having to fight long queues. When you do need to shop in department stores, be sure to go as soon as the stores open, when they're likely to be less crowded.
- 'Buy it when you see it' is a good rule of thumb. Make all types of gift-buying (even Christmas) a year-round project.

If you wait, you may have difficulty finding the item which seemed so perfect when you saw it a few months ago.

• Shopping by mail or phone is a time-saver. That item you saw while flipping through a catalogue may solve the dilemma of what to give your dad for Father's Day. And if the gift must be sent elsewhere, ask the shop or mail-order house to do it for you.

• Make sure you have a good stock of wrapping paper and tags for use at any time.

• Keep extra gifts on hand for unexpected needs. Stock up on exotic mustards, spices, jams and vinegars which can be attractively packed in a basket or box for a handy, last-minute gift.

• Consider gifts that don't require shopping: a magazine subscription (roll up a current issue and put a bow around it); tickets to the theatre, a concert, or sports event; membership in a local museum; a handwritten card informing the person of something you've set up for them – a massage, a class, a visit to a palm reader or psychic; an IOU offering to babysit, or run an errand.

If you implement these suggestions, then what happened to my cousin won't happen to you. At the last minute, she realised that she hadn't purchased a gift for her friend's birthday. Then she remembered an unopened bottle of fine wine she had received as a gift a few months before. How embarrassed she was when the present was opened and her friend commented that it was the exact same gift that she had given my cousin for her last birthday!

# 41: Handbag

You *should* have an organised handbag. It's a nuisance to have to take several moments to fish for a pen, and it's nothing short of dangerous not to be able to put your hands on your car or house keys quickly at night.

First, you'll need a well-made, functional bag. Choose one with pockets and zippered compartments for categorising your belongings. (Ideally, look for a bag that will double as a brief-case.) Stay away from a formless bag, as its contents will scatter everywhere within it and you'll constantly be hunting for what you need.

You may want to select a nylon or vinyl bag for wet weather. The contents will stay dry and it can be easily wiped off once you're at home or in the office.

What to carry? Keep it simple. Here are the necessities and some tips for each:

- *Wallet.* Categorise your money by denomination, small bills first. If you have a wallet with two sections for change, put large coins in one side and ten pences for telephone calls in the other.

  A wallet/card case combination is easier to manage; however, you do run the risk of losing everything if it's stolen.

- *Keys.* Keep them in a pocket or compartment within your bag so they are easily accessible. Identify them by number or colour-code, but *don't* put your name and address on the chain.

- *Day planner.* Use only one appointment book, and carry this with you at all times (see Chapter 8).

- *Small telephone directory.* Carry frequently called telephone numbers here.

- *Business-card case.* Keep your business cards where they can be easily located. At a business gathering, slip it in your pocket for greater convenience.

- *Pen and paper* (or small spiral notebook). Handy for jotting down notes and things to do.

- *Reading material.* Always have something with you in case you encounter an unexpected delay.

- *Small bag or purse.* This can serve one of three purposes: (1) Use it as a bag within a bag. At lunch, transfer valuables, money, keys and your diary to the purse and leave your big bag at the office. (2) Use it as a cosmetics bag. (3) Use it to hold receipts, business cards, and other items given to you during the day.

## Take along for the unexpected

- *On-the-go survival kit.* In your cosmetic bag or in another small pouch, pack a safety pin or two, Band-Aids, packaged moist towelettes, lip balm, tissues, aspirin, and needle and thread.

- *Stockings.* An extra pair comes in handy when the ones you're wearing run on the way to an important function. Roll them into a small ball and store in a small plastic bag to keep from snagging in your handbag.

- *Paper towels.* On a day when rain is predicted, slip in a few extra paper towels or a hand towel to help dry off rain or snow from your face and hands if you get soaked. (If you're wearing boots that day, carry your shoes in a plastic bag with a drawstring, available at some shoe stores.)

Make a habit of sorting through your handbag daily. Take out notes, receipts, and information gathered while out; process them; and make sure your bag is re-supplied for the next day.

Though it may be difficult to believe, there are a number of smart, well-groomed women who *never* carry a handbag. They trim down what they want to have with them and carry all their valuables in a few select pockets or in the tiniest purse. It's something to consider anyway!

# 42: Briefcase

When you travel the streets of a big city, where people walk or use public transport, you begin to realise that men and women use their briefcases to carry *everything:* I've seen people carrying their lunches, their laundry, and even their pets. Some people pack their cases so full that they lean to one side as they carry it.

The most important thing to remember about a briefcase is that its primary purpose is to transport items (usually papers) from one place to another. It is not a suitcase; it is not a storeroom; it is not a place to pack everything you were afraid to leave behind. It is your briefcase. Pack it carefully and it will serve you well.

## Shopping for a briefcase

- Basically, briefcases come in two styles: a hard-sided suitcase type and an expandable type. Personal preference (or the style carried by people in your industry) should dictate which style you choose. However, remember that the expandable type tends to be lighter, though it doesn't always preserve papers as well as the hard-sided style since there's a tendency to overstuff it.

- Look for a briefcase which totally seals so that papers don't get wet in rain or snow.

- A good briefcase has pockets and at least one zippered inside compartment where you can put your belongings. Some briefcases have sections specifically designed to hold items such as pens, calculators, and the like.

- If a style you like doesn't have inner pockets or compartments, you can buy a small zippered travel bag or transparent pencil case to serve this purpose.

- Many people like a pocket on the outside where they can slip their newspaper or magazine for reading in transit.

- Expandable briefcases sometimes come with removable

shoulder straps. This can be a real plus for easy hands-free carrying. If that style doesn't work well for you during the business week, consider looking for an inexpensive one with a shoulder strap for travel. Being able to toss the briefcase on your shoulder makes it easier to handle your hand luggage.

• Many women find that having a briefcase which doubles as a handbag is an additional convenience.

## What to carry

• Here are some suggested items to have along. For convenience, they are broken down into categories:

*Must have*
* Pad of paper
* Business cards
* Diary and address book (to have with you at all times)

* Pen or pencil with rubber
* Reading material

*Would like to have*
* Calculator
* Extra file folders
* Envelopes
* A few stamps

* Paperclips
* Post-it notes
* Highlighter

*Might come in handy*
* Small Dictaphone machine
* Ruler
* Small stapler
* Scissors (for cutting out articles)
* Small sewing kit, such as the ones provided by some hotels (Even men should have on hand a way to repair a torn seam!)
* Extra set of keys
* Stockings (roll and store in a small plastic bag)

* Tiny torch
* Nailfile and clipper
* Aspirin and Band-Aids
* Moist towelettes

• All small items (pen, stamps, aspirin, sewing kit) should be kept in the compartments of your briefcase (or in small travel bags) for accessibility. Keep personal items in one compartment; desk supplies in another.

- Be certain that all papers you carry are put in their own file folder and labelled appropriately. (Some people prefer to use manila envelopes.) Within the case, folders can be in chronological order according to the stops you'll be making or in alphabetical order.

## *Other tips*

- Make certain that what you've put into your briefcase to take home with you gets taken out each night. I once knew a man who lugged heavy books and papers to and from his office each day, never once taking them out. In the end he probably didn't even fool himself into thinking he was busy. The only bonus he got for his hard work was strong muscles.
- If you have a business meeting, make a list of what you'll need. Pack your briefcase according to the list. If your list is handy, you'll have an easy way to do a last-minute cross-check to see that you're ready for the meeting.
- Your briefcase should be thoroughly reorganised at least once a week. Re-supply as needed and be certain that items such as your calculator are in good working order. Don't forget to clean out old papers.

# 43: How to Stop Losing Things

Though everyone has left an umbrella in the cab, misplaced a favourite pen, or dropped a glove somewhere, far more often we are frustrated at losing something because we *know* it's right here at home — if only we could find it!

One client was fairly efficient about most things, but she didn't have a system for items she used occasionally. Every trip to the library was preceded by a frustrating search of the house for the place where she had last put her library card.

The old saying 'A place for everything and everything in its place' takes the misery out of losing things. Here are some simple ways to make it work for you.

## *Don't scatter — categorise*

- Items used frequently should be placed within easy reach.

- Infrequently used items should be stored away so they don't clutter up the storage areas for more frequently needed things.

- Items that are alike should be kept together (all stamps, paper, envelopes, and pens or pencils should be stored in or near your desk; hairclips and combs should have a special box or drawer in your dressing-table).

- Items used together should be stored together. For example, establish a bag where you keep all items for a trip to the beach.

- Items should be stored near where they are used (exercise equipment should be kept in the room where you use it; extra tote bags should be near the front door).

- How to make it work? When you're finished with something, put it back in its place right away.

## *Establish a permanent home for frequently used one-and-only's*

Here are two examples:

- *Keys.* A special hook, drawer, or bowl on a counter near the door is a good place for them. *Always* put them there!
- *Glasses.* If you mainly wear them for desk work, keep them in your briefcase or in your desk drawer. If you wear them for driving, keep them in your handbag or near the front door.

## *Storage tips*

- Use colour-coding or written labels on boxes for items stored on deep or high shelves. Label everything!
- Egg cartons, film tubes, small plastic drawer units (for make-up, etc.) or even homemade drawer partitions fashioned from cardboard can be a great help in categorising small things. Be imaginative!
- Establish a shelf or box for 'give away' items. Add to it as you find things you're tempted to throw out.
- Create a gift drawer or shelf so you have a designated spot for presents you buy ahead of time.
- Junk drawers are a real trap! Don't even consider having one.

## *Borrowed trouble*

Who hasn't lost countless books (and other possessions) to well-meaning friends who beg to take something home with them 'for just a few days.' The following helps:

- Put bookplates in books and stickers on other possessions to identify you clearly as the owner.
- In your Household Notebook, jot down the borrower's name, the date, and the item. If you do a lot of lending, create a file called Borrowing and Lending and keep the information there.

# 44: Organising Your Partner

'It's time my husband started making my life easier — I'm tired of picking up after him.' Or: 'My wife is so disorganised she even forgets to put the milk back in the refrigerator — we need help!' These are common sentiments I hear over and over in the seminars I conduct across the country.

What's more, I can identify with what it's like to live with someone who has a completely different approach to organisation. My husband enjoys making lists, and occasionally makes lists of lists. There are many times, though, when he forgets or loses them — leaving him at a loss for the day!

When it comes to organising your spouse, tolerance will have to be the order of the day. You won't survive as a couple if you try totally to reform him or her. Helpful resolves are the following:

- I respect his/her right to live the way he or she is most comfortable.

- I reserve the right to request certain changes so that his/her sloppiness or disorganisation no longer affects me or impedes the overall functioning of the household.

For example, I am more efficient than my husband at getting ready for things, so when we go to our weekend home, I'm responsible for all the packing; he's responsible for bringing the keys and loading and unloading the car. Rather than argue that I am doing most of the work, I simply accept what he *can* do in this situation. Then in other parts of our life, such as with grocery shopping, he does the lion's share of the work.

So after you've tried yelling, pleading, and other desperate tactics, think 'compromise', and improve what you can by using the following tips:

## Establishing a system

- Coordinate schedules. Establish at least two nights (such as

192

Wednesday and Sunday) when you sit down together and compare diaries. Make certain that each of you records the plans that affect you both.

- Provide him or her with a specific space so that his or her habits have less effect on you. Separate desks, shelves, cupboards, and suitcases are a good investment.

- A colour-coding system will help identify towels, toothbrushes, and cups.

- When it comes to household chores, ask for his/her input and you'll get more cooperation. A discussion may reveal that he hates to vacuum but doesn't mind doing the dishes. If you don't mind vacuuming, you can each do what you feel is a tolerable chore and thus avoid an argument.

- Divide tasks fairly. Each of you can take certain chores or parts of chores. For example, for a dinner party, let her do the shopping and you do the cooking. A task chart of what must be done each week or day by day will sort out responsibilities.

## *Hoping for modest reform*

- Set a good example. You can't force organisation, but you can encourage it.

- Inspire your partner. If your desk is constantly clear, he or she may be interested in learning from you.

- Communicate. Show him/her exactly where things belong. How do you want the health records filed so that you can find them again? Where do the out-of-season clothes belong? How should the medicine chest be arranged?

- Don't become a personal butler. If you always do the picking up, your partner has no reason to do it. It may be as simple as a lesson. Your husband may simply not know how to fold a sweater. Or your wife might not understand the importance of setting up a personal property inventory.

- Give positive reinforcement. It can help! But, a word or warning . . . Inspire, but don't seek total reform!

# 45: Wardrobe Shopping for Women

Have you ever made a shopping excursion where you walked into a store and became so confused and overwhelmed you turned around and walked out again?

Or have you ever gone shopping, intending to buy one red sweater and walked out with two instead—one green and one blue?

Have you ever come home with a terrific skirt only never to wear it because you didn't take time to shop for the 'perfect' blouse to go with it?

Everyone has mistakes hanging in their wardrobes ... the dress you bought to wear 'when I lose some weight', or the outfit which 'really isn't me after all ...'

But when the 'mistakes' in the cupboard outnumber the rest of your clothes, you know you're doing something wrong. It's time to re-think your shopping methods.

With thought and planning, you can build a coordinated wardrobe which will give you more outfits, with fewer purchases, than you have now. Here's how:

## Planning your new wardrobe

- Consider your budget. This will help you keep your shopping goals in perspective and force you to focus on what you really need. For example, in order to build a good wardrobe for work, you may not be able to add new casual clothes this autumn, but those can be the first thing you buy in the spring.

- Coordination is the key to a successful wardrobe. To achieve this, you will need to build your wardrobe around a colour scheme. Begin by choosing two major colours in which you look good. The two colours (e.g. peach and brown) should work well together so that the items you buy will easily coordinate. That way you'll have twice as many outfits from the same number of pieces.

- Weed through your current wardrobe. Take everything out of your cupboard, drawers, and shelves (see Chapter 23). *Discard items you haven't worn in the past two years.* (Honestly, if you haven't worn it after several years, you probably never will . . .) With the other items, ask: 'Is this still fashionable? Do I look good in it?' (Don't guess. Try it on.) 'Do I still *like* it?'

- Of the remaining items decide which ones you want to use as a base for your new wardrobe. Select the clothing that makes you look terrific and feel comfortable. You may have a wonderful jacket and blouse, or one good suit you'd like to use as your base item. Keep your work and lifestyle requirements in mind.

- Make a list of what you need to fill in with your basic wardrobe items and put this list in your Household Notebook (see Chapter 22) under 'To Buy'. The list will give you an action plan for your shopping trip and should help you avoid impulse-buying. (Remember, that's how you gained most of the mismatches you have now!)

- Organise your list into categories (shoes, sweaters, accessories, etc.).

- Look through magazines and tear out pictures of fashions you like. Paste these in your Notebook as a reminder.

## Planning the shopping trip

- Plan to devote the better part of a day to your first shopping trip. A couple of hours just isn't enough time. (But *don't* shop so long that you get over tired. It will affect your decision making.)

- Think ahead about where you'd like to shop. Where are your favourite shops? Plan to restrict each trip to a single geographical area so you can focus your energies on accomplishing the task at hand.

- Of course, you'll need to take a list with you. Some people have chosen a portable size for their Household Notebook because they like to carry it with them; thus they have their list close at hand. I usually recommend you carry just the appropriate pages with you. Or you can go through the Household Notebook list and transfer pertinent information (what you plan to shop for on this expedition) to your diary 'To Do' list which you should have with you at all times.

## *Getting ready*

- Wear an outfit (such as separates) which will simplify trying clothes on in the store. That way you won't have to take a dress off if you're only trying on a blouse. If you're shopping for a new item to coordinate with something you already have, try to wear part of your basic wardrobe (the skirt? the blouse and jacket?) to save carrying it.

- If you're choosing a skirt to go with a blouse and jacket you already have and you decide not to wear them, you'll need to take the blouse and jacket with you. It can be difficult to remember the lines of clothing well enough to know if the 'look' will be right once you have on all three pieces.

- Avoid wearing anything that has lots of buttons; don't wear a turtleneck pullover that can be hard to pull on over your head, high boots (especially a boots-and-trousers combination), or lots of jewellery which can get tangled.

- Wear a hairstyle which keeps the hair out of your face but can be neatened easily once you've finished in the dressing room.

- Wear (or take) the bra you'll be wearing with the type of outfit for which you're shopping. If you're trying on evening wear, be sure to take the appropriate lingerie.

- Choose comfortable shoes to wear that are easy to slip on and off.

- If you will be having a dress or skirt hem adjusted, take (or wear) the shoes you intend to wear with the outfit. (If you need just a rough idea of how the heel height will affect the dress, carry along only one of the shoes.)

- Take a lightweight shoulder bag. A bag tends to get in the way when you're combing through racks and carrying clothing into the dressing room. A heavy one also makes you tire faster simply because you're carrying the added weight.

## *When shopping*

- Think coordination. Aim to create a variety of outfits from three or four pieces.

- Consider the seasonality of clothes. Some fabrics such as wool can be worn all year round. They are easy to fold, don't crease, and look smart all day. It also simplifies shopping because there will be less need for seasonal shopping.

- Go for the classics. If you want to be stylish, try to adapt a classic outfit to the fashions of the season. For example, extra shoulder pads can help give a fashionable big-shouldered look to a classic blouse or sweater with the right cut. Or add this year's accessories to a more conservative outfit you already own.

- Try on everything! Just because a sweater is marked medium doesn't mean it will fit *you* properly. I know several women who buy without trying on, but if I dared to do that, I'd spend the rest of my life on returning things.

- If you find a pair of trousers, blouse, or shoes you look great in, consider buying two. If it's perfect for you and you can use more than one colour of the same style, it's a good investment.

- Judge each article of clothing based on how you *feel* in it. Even if it's a beautiful outfit, you've got to look well in it and feel good about yourself.

- Steer clear of hard-to-wear accessories. Bows and ties and additional accessories can become difficult to keep in place through an entire business day. Keep that in mind as you shop.

- Check the garment care label. Is the item going to be more trouble that it's worth to take care of?

- Avoid impulse purchases. Stick to your list.

- Don't buy what you don't need or won't wear again.


## *Other tips*

- Shop by mail. This is especially helpful for items where fit is not important such as when shopping for a scarf, tote, or beach cover-up.

- Shop alone. While everyone likes support, too many second opinions may encourage you to make purchases you'd never dream of making on your own. It's also a real time-waster when you have your mind set on getting things done.

# 46: Wardrobe Shopping for Men

Most men would prefer to do anything other than shop for clothing. That's probably why the men's department of most stores is right at street level. Maybe the tradespeople assume that they're doing well if a fellow has stepped in the door — why push their luck by expecting him to go much further!

While I can't promise that this chapter will make you love shopping, what I can promise is that there is a way to simplify the system and make it as efficient as possible. And remember, the more efficient you are, the less time you'll have to spend at it and the fewer trips you'll have to make!

## Planning your wardrobe shopping

- Assess your clothing needs. Most executives find that the following basics meet their needs:
  - ★ Three suits — in neutral colours, two plain and one in a classic pattern
  - ★ One jacket in a neutral, solid colour for maximum versatility
  - ★ Trousers in grey or brown wool; they should be lighter or darker than the jacket
  - ★ Seven shirts. Because the suits and blazer are in basic colours, shop for shirts which coordinate with everything. A supply of at least seven shirts allows for one for each day of the business week with a couple left over for travel or for delays at the laundry.
  - ★ An assortment of ties which coordinate with the above (Vary the look of your outfits by mixing and matching shirts and ties.)
  - ★ Seven pairs of socks in grey, black, navy, and brown
  - ★ Shoes — one black pair, one brown, and one beige or burgundy
- For summer, repeat the basic colours you've chosen for your winter suits but in lighter-weight fabrics so that all your

shirts and ties will coordinate with both your summer and winter wardrobes.

- As you take stock of your current wardrobe, give away anything that is frayed or beginning to look worn, and *discard anything you haven't worn in the last two years.*
- Also note if you are low on underwear or casual clothing, and add those items to your shopping list.
- Organise your list into categories (casual clothing, dress shirts, accessories) to simplify your time in the shop.
- Set a budget.

## Simplifying the shopping trip

- To avoid confusion about your correct sizes, record your suit size, collar measurement, shoe and hat size, as well as waist and trouser length measurements on a card to be carried in your wallet. (Give a copy to your wife, mother, or girlfriend to receive gifts that fit from now on!)
- Decide where you would like to shop. Some men prefer to go to one department store and get their shopping done all at one time. Others feel overwhelmed by large shops and prefer to buy from smaller specialist shops.
- If you want to visit more than one shop to make comparisons, limit the number to three. Going to more won't necessarily bring you better prices or merchandise, and it *will* wear you out. If possible, choose shops that are in close proximity to each other to make the excursion as easy as possible.
- Select shops that fit your image.
- Shop at a store where the sales help is reliable and professional. Try to develop a relationship with a salesperson, as it can save you time and money. Have the person call you when a specific raincoat in your size comes in or when the annual sale begins. If you become a loyal customer, you may even be able to phone ahead and have some items put aside for you. Or you may simply want to call to be certain that your favourite salesperson is in.
- In order to shop efficiently, it is best to go to the shops at a time when they are least likely to be crowded. The fewer the people, the faster you can be in and out. Listed below, in order of preference, are some possible shopping times:

★A business day right after the shop opens
★Just after a shop opens on Saturday morning
★Evenings
★Middle of the business day.

## What to wear

- Wear clothing appropriate to what you want to buy. If you're buying a jacket, suit or raincoat, be sure to wear a shirt, tie, and a jacket so you can get a feel for how the outfit will look.
- Proper shoes are important for making certain that trouser length is correct. Proper socks are important if you're buying shoes.
- Go over your list and be sure to take it with you.

## What to buy

- Don't buy on impulse. Stick to your list.
- Plan to coordinate your entire ensemble on the day you shop for a suit. Buy the tie, the pocket handkerchief, and the shirt that go with it. It's hard to coordinate by trying to remember what you bought, and it's inconvenient to take a suit with you on a future shopping trip.
- Buy classic designs. The clothing lasts, and it won't go out of style as quickly. If you want to look trendy, do it by adding a stylish shirt or tie.
- Don't depend on designer labels. They don't always mean quality.
- Look for quality in make and fabric.
- Try on anything of which you're unsure of the fit. It will save you the tedium of having to return it.
- With items such as underwear or sports shirts, buy in bulk if it's a good fit or if the items are on sale.

## Wardrobe tips

- If you anticipate having trouble remembering which items can be worn together, set up a coded system showing how your wardrobe can be coordinated. Place into groups all garments that go together and assign a letter (A,B,C) to each group. Then mark or sew that letter on the inside label of each garment. (A salesperson might be interested in helping you by listing which items coordinate if you buy from him regularly or if you've just bought several coordinated purchases.) This sytem will automatically simplify dressing in the morning.

- Men's wardrobes can benefit from a double row of rods (one high, one lower). One can be for trousers and shirts; the other can hold suits and jackets.

- Use shoe trees to help shoes keep their shape.

- Purchase a tie rack to hang on the back of your wardrobe door. There are many good styles available, so base your decision on what will work well for you. Having your ties conveniently displayed will make selection easier in the morning.

- Roll underwear, socks and belts for easy storage. (Don't ball socks one inside the other; it stretches the elastic.)

- A light which goes on as the wardrobe door opens is a handy luxury.

- At the end of the season, check all your clothing for mending or possible discarding. Have everything laundered or cleaned before putting it in storage until next season.

## Clothing care

- Each night, inspect your suit, shirt and tie for stains, tears, pulls, or lost buttons. If repairs are needed, get them done before returning the item to your wardrobe.

- Frequent dry cleaning takes the life out of clothing, so clean only as needed.

- Buy a steamer to take creases and wrinkles out of suits and trousers. It's ideal for home use and perfect for travel.

- Laundries seem to thrive on breaking buttons, so be sure to check your shirt the night before to avoid early morning panic over a broken button. Keep a supply of extra buttons on hand so that they can be repaired as needed.

# Section 7
## ~
# Children

# 47: Pregnancy Checklist

The pregnant woman who expects to spend 50 hours a week working, entertain friends, volunteer for committee work, and still bake homemade bread is making a big mistake. You can do anything, but not everything!

Some women are very fortunate and report having excess energy throughout pregnancy; however, more women find that sometimes they just can't quite keep up with their regular schedule. For some, it comes at the beginning of the pregnancy when nausea and an increased need for sleep are common. In my own case (and that of many others), it was towards the end of pregnancy when I had to slow down. I had made a big effort to get everything done well in advance, and I was so glad I did. Towards the end of my pregnancy, I was confined to bed for a brief period, and I would have been frantic if there had been many things left to take care of. (I will also warn you of what all mothers learn firsthand: with a newborn baby, it seems you are busy *all* day, but if you had to describe it, it would either sound silly or it would *not* sound very time-consuming. But believe me, it is!)

At any rate, you need to start preparing as soon as your pregnancy is confirmed. Your main goal is to be ready when your baby arrives, and that means taking a systematic approach to pregnancy by setting your priorities now — what you want to do; what you need to do.

Here are some ways to handle the many responsibilities ahead.

## First three months: to do

- Make the following decisions about medical care, keeping in mind that each decision will affect the other:
  - ★ Select hospital and discuss birth procedures with your G.P. and/or consultant.
  - ★ Discuss with your doctor whether you should have an amniocentesis test (usually given to women over 35 during the fifteenth to eighteenth week of pregnancy to determine possible genetic abnormalities in the foetus).

- Start thinking about how to rearrange your home for the baby. Will you need to move or can you reorganise? Consider your options so you'll have time to act before the baby arrives.
- Begin a 'Household Projects' page in your Household Notebook (see Chapter 22). List anything you want to do to get the house in order before the baby is born: reorganise cupboards, clean rugs, wax floors, buy washing machine, and so forth.
- Revise budget to accommodate new family member.
- Organise family files and records and start a 'Pregnancy' file, which includes articles and information on pregnancy, childbirth and parenting.

## First three months: to buy

- Select new bras with good support (you'll want them!).
- Visit a bookshop and buy some books on pregnancy, childbirth, breast-feeding and infant care.

## First three months: to find out

- Call the personnel department of your company and inquire about benefits and leave-of-absence policy. Some firms require that you work until two to four weeks before your delivery date to qualify for benefits.

## First three months: to enjoy

- Take advantage of leisurely weekend mornings and sleep late!

## Second three months: to do

- Many women find this the ideal time to share the good news with family and friends. (Most miscarriages occur in the first three months, so you're less likely to have problems now.)
- Discuss your preferred leave-of-absence schedule with your boss.

- Have amniocentesis, if you plan to do so.

- If you plan to move or reorganise, try to complete as much of the project as possible now.

- If you intend to breast-feed, start to prepare your nipples now. Check with your doctor or consult a book on breast-feeding for instructions.

- Most new parents like to have extra assistance when the baby comes. With whom would you feel most comfortable — Your mother? Sister? A nurse? If you decide on a relative, discuss it now.

- If you plan to use a nurse, ask friends to recommend one or ask them to recommend a good nursing agency. If you find a real gem, reserve her now. (Most agencies will take bookings on a few days notice, so you still have plenty of time.)

- If you have other children at home, plan for their care while you'll be in the hospital.

- Borrow any baby clothes you can. Make a list of each item you've borrowed and to whom it belongs. The list will also help you in a few months when you go shopping because you'll know what you don't need to buy. Wash the clothing and put it away.

- Start a Gifts-We'd-Love-to-Receive list and tell people exactly what you want when asked.

- Start your list of potential names for the baby.

## Second three months: to buy

- Shop for (or borrow) maternity clothing. Don't forget about a coat or jacket.

## Second three months: to find out

- Register for childbirth classes, which will start in your seventh or eighth month.

## Second three months: to enjoy

- Sneak off for a wonderful vacation with your husband!

## *Third three months: to do*

- Visit your dentist (no X-rays).
- If you plan to leave work early, make the necessary preparations for a smooth departure.
- Attend childbirth classes with your partner.
- Begin to decorate the baby's room (paint walls, lay carpet, hang curtains, etc.).
- Take a tour of the hospital and learn about the check-in system. (You may also want to ask if you'll be allowed to take photographs in the delivery room.)
- Prepare a list of tasks that will need to be done while you're in the hospital, such as calls to spread the good news and to arrange for deliveries. (Be sure to list all phone numbers!) Also include information your partner may need to function at home without you.
- Consider changes to be made in your insurance policies and wills, and choose a guardian for your child. Discuss any changes with your insurance representative and your solicitor, and arrange for them to take effect after the baby's birth.

## *Third three months: to buy*

- Shop for baby furniture.
- Shop for baby's layette (clothes, blankets, accessories) and arrange for delivery.
- Buy a huge stock of nappies and all baby's bathroom needs.

## *Third three months: to find out*

- Check with the hospital or local National Childbirth Trust organiser about childcare classes and enrol.
- Book a nurse if you decide to have one. Give the agency your due date. They'll provide you with someone whether you're early or late.

### Third three months: to enjoy

- Pamper yourself! Get a haircut, enjoy a manicure, read a good book.

## Last month: to do

- Cook ahead and freeze meals for your homecoming.
- Prepare suitcase for the hospital.
- Pack prepared childbirth bag.
- Start interviewing now if you'll need full-time household help when you come home.

## Last month: to buy

- Buy nursing bras if you plan to breast-feed.

## Last month: to call

- Confirm furniture and/or layette deliveries.
- Confirm childcare arrangements for children at home.

## Last month: to enjoy

- Celebrate the fact that you are prepared.

## At the hospital: to telephone

- Notify nurse or nursing agency.
- Give the newspaper details for birth announcement.

Rest and enjoy the baby!

# 48: Post-Pregnancy: Organisation after the Baby is Born

There is no time that is more disorganised or confusing than after coming home with a new baby. There are generally extra people around, no one is following their normal schedule, and everyone is simply basing their actions on what they anticipate the baby's schedule will be — and of course, the little character usually does his or her best to surprise everyone!

I don't think I knew the *true* meaning of 'busy' until our daughter Julia was born. My little half-pint had me going in circles! To cope, I had to develop a way to do all my regular activities — only faster (now I shower more quickly, have a simpler haircut, and do an easier makeup routine). And I had to figure out how to do all the childcare chores while still saving time just to be with my baby. It's not easy, but it's possible — eventually.

The art of getting through the early days lies largely in simply remaining flexible enough to cope with what comes; however, there are some measures you can take to help things along.

## If you haven't done so already

Ideally, you will have taken care of many of the following points prior to your baby's birth:

- Buy one or two good books on baby care. (Get recommendations from friends.) You won't have time to read many, but a voice of authority illuminating what the midwife or health visitor told you about early feedings, putting an infant to sleep, or coping with first sniffles can be enormously reassuring.
- If planning to breast-feed, set up a support network. Get the number of your local La Leche League and talk to friends who have breast-fed successfully.

209

- Stock the freezer with breads and pre-cooked dinners for the first days at home.
- With your partner's help, prepare a list — complete with phone numbers — of all people who should be called as soon as the baby is born.
- At the office, stay on top of your work, and establish systems so that the staff can run things in your absence.
- Change your will (or have one drawn up) and change your insurance policy.

## After the birth

- Notify close friends and relatives. To make it simpler, ask some of the first people you call phone other people.
- Arrange for a circumcision, if appropriate.
- Arrange for a christening or naming ceremony.
- Select godparents, guardians.
- Send announcements.

## The early days at home

- Don't even attempt to get organised right away. Just do nothing for awhile and give yourself time to get back on track. (Babies don't know about organisation and they really don't care — they just want you to be available when you're needed!)
- There's nothing wrong with asking people not to come over right away. Give yourself time to adjust and rest. Just at the time you need all your energy for mothering, you're also physically and emotionally drained.
- Accept help from anyone who offers. And don't be afraid to ask for help. This is one time when people are only too glad to lend a hand.
- Relax whenever you can, during the baby's nap or while someone else is with him or her. Only if you are well rested and calm will you be able to enjoy your baby!
- Keep your list of announcements and use it to note down gifts as they arrive. Then check off each as the thank-you note is sent.

- Write several thank-you notes each day so that it doesn't become overwhelming.
- Plan to cook dinners in the morning or arrange for others to cook.
- Start thinking about what type of household help you will need, but wait to hire until after you've evaluated what your needs will be.
- Schedule your own doctor's appointment for a postpartum check-up (usually at six weeks, but ask your doctor just to be sure).
- Start a photo album.
- Start a tape of baby's first sounds including crying, laughing, babbling and cooing.
- Check out support groups for mothers and/or fathers through your local National Childbirth Trust branch or hospital. Having the opportunity to speak with other parents and share information during this transitional time is very helpful.
- Arrange time for yourself whenever possible. Take the baby's rest time for yourself, and book a temporary babysitter (or call upon a relative or friend) when you need more than an hour or so off.

## *Starting the day*

One of the most common pitfalls new mothers face is when to get dressed. I constantly hear, 'And there it was noon, and I was still in my nightgown . . . ' Here's what to do.

- If your baby takes an early nap (many go right back to sleep after they have their first feeding), get up and use that time for showering, getting dressed, and having breakfast. If you're dressed and feeling somewhat organised, it is easier to face the day. You can use other naps for getting the additional rest you need.
- Not all babies are so cooperative about taking that early nap. Try putting the infant in an infant seat and letting him or her sit on the floor of the bathroom and watch you shower and dry your hair, and the like. If your baby becomes conditioned to the fact that this is one 10-minute period when you have something else to do, he or she will generally make

the most of that time looking around — and 'plotting' how to keep you busy for the rest of the day!

## *Organising food-related supplies*

- If your baby is formula-fed, prepare all the bottles at one time so that you're set for the day.
- Always clean the bottles after use so that rotation is easy.
- Store baby teats and caps in a closed jar or tin so you'll always have pre-sterilised equipment handy. Put used items in another pot (a bowl or another jar) so that you'll know what is ready for sterilising.
- Have one shelf or cupboard for all of baby's things (bottles, warming dish, spoon, cups).
- In the fridge, have one section for baby food so that it's easy to find what's open and available.

## *Laundry and bathtime tips*

- Always keep up with the baby's wash so that you don't run out of babygrows, T-shirts, and bibs.
- Have at least three sets of cot sheets: one on the bed, one in the laundry, and a fresh one in the drawer.
- Soak clothing immediately after a stain. It's easier to keep it white and fresh that way. (Have a bucket on hand in which to throw soiled items.)
- Select easy-to-wear clothes with poppers in all the important places (for nappy changes and for extending the neck opening). Once you've tried to dress a screaming baby, you'll be especially glad. Also, always buy big. They grow so quickly!
- Save trips at bathtime by using a plastic box or trolley to store baby soap, shampoo, lotion, powder and toys.
- Buy canisters meant for storing flour, sugar and tea to hold baby items (cotton, ribbons, nail scissors, thermometer, etc.).
- For after bath, put the bottle of baby lotion in hot water. The lotion will be warm when you rub it on the baby's skin.
- Put towels in a warm drier for a few minutes. Remove just before the bath. It's a wonderful way to get baby dry!

## Getting out of the house

At no time is a parent's organisational skill more sorely tested than when trying to get out of the house with a baby (or a child of any age for that matter!) in tow.

- Always have a pre-packed nappy bag ready to go. Choose one that is soft and featherweight. Velcro fastenings make for easy opening and closing. Outside pockets help you find what you need (wipes, tissues, money, or keys) quickly. A vinyl inside makes for easy cleaning. Always re-pack it as soon as you get home. What goes inside? Carry a change of clothing, a blanket, extra formula, a package of teats and caps, plastic bags with ties for soiled nappies, several sheets of paper towels, moist towelettes and ointment for nappy changes, small bottles of lotion and powder, and at least two extra nappies. Also carry a puppet or some attention-getting toy to get you through a rough time. It sounds like a trunkful, but it's really not so bad – once you're used to it!

- If you have an appointment to go to the doctor or to meet a friend, leave an *extra* 30 minutes for last-minute 'surprises' (and babies will always provide them!), such as an extra nappy change, a longer-than-usual feeding, or vomiting – or all of the above and more.

## How to get non-baby work done

If you're trying to accomplish something during the early days of motherhood (job search, work-related project, or even just finishing thank-you notes), you really can't count on getting much done during the baby's nap. Sleep patterns often change from day-to-day, and often what you need during that period is a good rest yourself. Here are some suggestions:

- Get back-up help. Consider your needs. Perhaps a babysitter one day a week will be enough, or you may need help three days a week. Establish a set routine with the sitter so that you have one person coming to you regularly. Then the baby will become accustomed to one person, you won't have to re-instruct every time, and you'll know that you will definitely have a specific time to accomplish what needs to be done. Schedule that time, for example:

Monday: Stay home to work.
Wednesday: Errands, food shopping, dentist appointment.
Friday: Stay home to work.

Be consistent or the time will slip away from you.

- Choose an area of the house in which to work, where you aren't in sight of the baby, and close the door. Try not to listen. If you've chosen well, your sitter should be given the authority to handle whatever comes up. If you teach your child that you'll come in at an especially loud wail, the baby will work very hard to wring out those mother-producing wails which bring you.
- Teach your sitter to schedule and organise. You may need to explain such management techniques as starting the washing machine before going out for a walk with the baby so that the laundry will be finished when she comes back in.
- When you've been out, plan to come home at least 15 minutes before the sitter has to leave to have time to hang up your coat, wash, change clothes, and put away your packages, so your home won't be in chaos for the rest of the day.

## Additional suggestions

- For night feedings, if you are not breast-feeding, set up a system with your mate so that each of you takes full duty every other night — doing all feedings and walking during that time. That way you each have one full night on — but one full night off for badly needed sleep.
- If you must leave after a nursing, get completely ready with make-up, stockings, and shoes, but put on a robe rather than your clothes. Then you can feed the baby without having to worry about milk getting on the outfit. As soon as you're finished with the feeding, you slip into your outfit and you're gone.
- Consider putting a telephone extension in the baby's room. It can be turned off during naps, and it's certainly handy when the phone rings during a nappy change.
- Or install an answering machine for those awkward moments.

# 49: Children's Rooms

When it comes to household organisation, one of the most difficult areas to keep well-organised is a child's room. Offspring of all ages are experts at creating chaos.

Obviously, picking up after the kids or nagging is no solution. The first step is to create an environment which is conducive to organisation. This involves letting your children's interests dictate the basic plan for the environment (so that the most interesting items are the most available) and then creating a system which allows a child to help maintain order.

## General planning

- The first thing to do is to re-think the use of the child's space and, if necessary, rearrange it so that his or her interests are taken into consideration. If he loves to build with blocks but they are difficult to get out and put away, you've automatically created a difficult activity to keep organised. Consider the use of play areas and set up the room accordingly. For your block builder, create a clear space in a corner of his room and store the blocks nearby. If your child is an avid reader, establish a seat near the bookcase and make sure there is good lighting. For a young artist, choose a place where you can put a child's table with art supplies nearby. If a three-year-old can take out (and put away) paper and crayons for herself, you've created an effective system.

- Though I have stressed the importance of colour-coding throughout the book nowhere is it more important than in a child's room. There are two practical uses for it:

  *In keeping belongings separate.* Amanda knows her toothbrush is red, so she always knows which toothbrush/towel/bathroom glass is hers.

  *In putting things away.* By using different coloured bins or painting shelves in different colours, you can create a system for your toddler to put toys away. No reading necessary! The dinosaur figures go on the green shelf, the blocks go on the red, and so on.

215

• Establish a spot where clutter is allowed on a temporary basis. No child should have to put away everything all the time. If your daughter wants to spread out all her doll's house toys in a pre-established corner of the room, that should be all right for several days. (Set up a system such as Monday and Thursday for cleaning up most projects.) Allow the spot to move occasionally. If the kids want to build a cardtable house in the living room for a night or two and the family won't be inconvenienced, they ought to be able to swap that mess for one in their room.

• For toddlers and pre-schoolers who mainly play with a variety of big toys, establish baskets or bins in each room, including the living room, dining room, and study where they can keep a few toys they like to play with. It makes cleaning in the room much easier, and the bins can be moved easily if company is to arrive. In addition, by moving the dining room bin into the living room, the kids get a whole new perspective on the toys!

• If you live in a home where the children have their own bedroom as well as playroom, reserve their rooms for special or new toys. Use the playroom as the main storage area. This simplifies tidying up time because everyone know that all toys go to the playroom; you needn't determine what goes to John's room and what goes to Adam's.

• Some families like to establish one room as 'off limits' (such as the parents' bedroom). While this shouldn't be overdone, it may be workable for some areas. Certainly, most parents should stipulate that, because of potential hazards, the bathrooms and kitchen are off limits for unsupervised play. Another possibility for preserving a room's neatness while still allowing your children some freedom might be to stipulate that certain rooms must be used as intended. Being in the living room is fine if a child wants to sit on the couch with his or her feet on a stool or the floor, but romping and climbing are forbidden.

## Storage tips

• Lower wardrobe hanging poles and hooks so that your children can reach them. This will make dressing and putting things away much easier.

- Keep toys where they are used. Bath toys should be in a plastic basket in the bathroom; toys for the sitting room might be in a bin or stored in a cupboard; outdoor toys should go on the back porch.

- Group together similar toys. All puzzles should be together; likewise all games, all stuffed animals.

- If you use shelves for storage, be sure they are fastened securely. Bookcases should be anchored as well. Active toddlers are prone to scaling any type of shelving.

- Use sketches or a catalogue photograph taped to a box to identify certain items. Children too young to read can easily identify the 'beads' box, if it has a picture of beads on the outside.

- Plastic boxes are good for storage. Make sure there are no sharp edges!

- Try a toy sheet for an infant's toys or for a toy which has a lot of pieces. Collect the toys (or pieces) on a sheet on which the child can play. When the child is done, simply fold up the sheet — toys and all — and put it away for the next time.

- Encourage children to take out only a few toys at a time. If they want to do puzzles, encourage them to put away the game first.

## Weeding out

- Automatically throw away any toy which becomes hazardous. If a part snaps off and there's a sharp edge, or if eyes on a stuffed animal cannot be secured and might come off and cause a child to choke, throw it away.

- Until your child is old enough to take care of his or her own room and keep it somewhat neat, you probably have the right to weed things out periodically — without his or her approval. After all, the clay sculpture her best friend gave her six months ago and the doll's shoe whose mate is missing really can't be saved for ever . . .

- Give your child the chance to make the decision to part with a toy. If you've noticed one hasn't been used for a while, you might ask if it's okay to give it away (to a hospital or a charity shop). Sometimes a child will surprise you with a 'yes'!

- If a part is lost (and it's not such a favourite toy that you are met with a flood of tears until you promise to replace the part), use that as a reason to throw a toy out.
- Favourite toys can often be mended. Contact your local toy shop or the manufacturer.
- Suggest that your child give away one toy when he or she receives a new one.
- Let your child help pack toys in a box for charity; talk about how happy another child will be to receive them.
- Rotate toys. If your child just can't part with some toys but you need to clear space, establish a 'surprise' bin and cycle some of the toys out for a while. Then if your child is at home sick or you feel trapped inside on a rainy day, you can get out the bin. Chances are, you'll both be in for a surprise at how much fun your child will have playing with the old toys. (If any toy doesn't catch the child's interest after being taken out of circulation for a while, toss it out.)
- Exchange toys. Perhaps your child and his friend would like to swap games (or puzzles or books) for a time. Specify a date when the toys should be returned (swapping for 'keeps' is hard at almost any age).

# 50: Teaching Children about Organisation

Parents who teach their children an organisational system and the value of it will have given their offspring a head start in life. The toddler will begin to learn responsibility and be better prepared to cope with the 'putting away' rules of nursery school. And as the child matures, he or she will be learning some basic organisational skills which will stand him in good stead for building lifelong work habits.

Organisation is a skill that *can* be learned. The earlier you start instilling in your children these habits and the benefits, the easier it will be for them.

With toddlers, the place to start is by having them help with the day-to-day toy clean-up. As they grow older, you'll want to teach them how to be responsible for their own room and have them help with specific tasks around the house. This will help promote a feeling of self-reliance and give them more control over their lives. Another important benefit of good organisational habits is when it comes to schoolwork.

## Cleaning up, toddler-style

Toddlers should learn that what comes out must go back. There are fun ways to encourage your child to help and still allow you to get the job done efficiently.

- Encourage your child to help with cleaning up, but don't overwhelm him or her. Request help with just one thing at a time. 'You pick up the doll's clothes; I'll do the books.'
- Sing while you work together.
- Ask, 'How quickly can we get this done?' Set the kitchen timer for five or ten minutes and see if you can get everything done before the bell rings.
- Make a game of it. Ask, 'Can you pick up all the stuffed animals and put them back before I finish with the blocks?'

219

## As they grow: taking responsibility for their own room

- Simplify a task according to age level. Teach a pre-schooler how to make a bed by standing at the head of the bed and pulling up the covers.

- Establish a standard so that your child knows what is expected. For example, you may care only that your eight-year-old pull the duvet over the bed — not that the sheets underneath be crease-free. Tell your child exactly what is expected.

- Label where everything goes (via colour-coding or written labels) so that your child knows what goes where.

- Allot a special drawer or shelf in the bathroom for their belongings.

- Suggest ways to get the job done pleasantly by putting on a favourite record, telling yourself a story, pretending to be Cinderella, or the like.

- Have a laundry basket in the child's room, and make him or her responsible for putting dirty clothes there. At a later date, you can teach children to be responsible for putting away as well. Show them how you want the clothes placed and in what drawers — but don't expect perfection!

- Help children build personal pride in their room. Let them have a hand in decorating it and praise them for the times when they are showing an interest in beautifying it (despite the fact that the two of you may have a different definition of 'beauty'!).

- Children usually get attention for *not* cleaning their room. Be sure to pay attention when they do.

## Taking on other responsibilities

- Set an example of planning and priorities by talking in those terms about everyday household events. For example, the child who can read can help plan a trip to the supermarket by reviewing the flapjack recipe and listing those ingredients that must be purchased before flapjacks can be made.

- Getting an older child to do household chores usually

involves constant reminding. You can establish a rota chart, which can help them determine what they are supposed to do on what day. A chart should list each family member's name, followed by the tasks for which he or she is currently responsible, and the day on which each is to be done.

• As your children mature, let them take charge of marking their own dates on the family calendar. You're the best judge of when each is ready for that responsibility.

• Check with your child about forthcoming events at school, so that no one misses a date because a note was lost. (The child is responsible, but you offer a system of cross-checking.)

## Teaching self-reliance

• Both mother and father should play active roles in the clearing up and organisational work of the home. The best way to teach is by example.

• Help children become more independent by teaching them how to tie their shoes, button their sweater, get their own snack, or operate the tape recorder. The more they can do, the better they'll feel about themselves, and the more organised you can be.

## Schoolwork and organisation

As a child begins to assume responsibility for schoolwork, organisation becomes more important than ever. The children who learn how to arrange their books, desks, lockers, and note-books will likely become more organised adults. For the present, however, being organised generally means finishing projects earlier (because of not having to look for things), and then having more time for fun.

• For schoolwork, provide your child with a well-lit, comfortable work area.

• Suggest that your child establish a colour-coding system for homework folders by subject. Most children enjoy a trip to the stationers to buy the necessary supplies, and the system will help them throughout the year.

- Teach your child how to label notebooks and arrange desk supplies.

- When you first see your child after school, ask about homework and discuss what the assignments are and about how long they should take. You can help them set up a time management system. If necessary, you can establish a reward such as 'After you finish you can watch half an hour of television . . .'

- If your child seems stuck, stop and help him or her plan steps to complete something (break a large task down into parts, etc.).

- Praise your child for work well done. Talk about what great progress he or she is making in developing positive work habits for later in life.

# 51: Travelling with Children

While the hours you spend on a plane or in a train or a car with your child may not be the highlight of your life, remember what someone once said: All places should be seen through a child's eyes. After all, it is the children who stop to notice the small details, and it is they who take the time to sit by a fountain rather than rushing from one museum to another. If you're brave enough to pack your youngsters and go, the chances are you'll have a wonderful time.

## General planning

- If possible, plan to travel during the baby or child's nap time. This can save you a lot of wear and tear at the beginning or end of a trip.
- Think through your child's day and make a checklist so you won't forget certain 'must haves' (blanket, washcloths, etc.). One woman I know had made a great list of clothing and bedding needs, but had neglected to note the everyday items such as nappies and bottles. Sure enough, she forgot the bottles — they were in the dishwasher!
- Take at least one full change of clothes in case of spills or travel sickness. (The younger the child, the more clothes you are likely to need. For an infant, take along two or three changes — the second set of back-up clothing can be lightweight so they are easy to pack, and you can add a sweater if it's chilly.) Pack separates when possible. That way if the shirt gets juice all over it, at least you don't have to change the trousers.
- Expect the unexpected. If you'll be in the car or on the plane or train for five hours, take enough nappies for ten to fifteen hours. (In your suitcase, be sure to pack nappies for your arrival so you don't immediately have to go shopping.)
- Take an adequate supply of plastic bags for nappies and rubbish. A nervous child can develop diarrhoea, and you

223

don't want to be caught short without a way to dispose of the nappies!

● Take any and all medications your child might need. Colds are a particular worry when travelling, so take along the remedies your doctor recommends. And if your child has a tendency to any illness, such as ear infections, also take any medication the doctor may have prescribed. There's nothing worse than being in a strange city and not having the necessary medicine in the middle of the night. Remember, anticipate the unexpected.

● For very young children, pack familiar toys and books so there will be something to give them the feeling of home. Ideally, pack these toys (all but the true favourites) about a week in advance so that they seem new but familiar at the same time. A few new toys are nice, but there's no need to overdo it. For entertainment at your destination, blow-up toys are wonderful because they pack so easily.

● If you're comfortable with your baby in a front-pack or a sling, be sure to plan on travelling with it. It makes you far more mobile than having to rely totally on using a pram or buggy.

● Buy a travel clothes-line so that you can wash light clothing by hand.

● If you are going away on business, bring someone to help out.

● Select a family-oriented hotel. If you're travelling to a foreign country, make certain that you'll have your own bath, and try to clarify what they mean by certain words such as 'suite'. One family expected a separate bedroom for the children and discovered that the 'bedroom' was an alcove which couldn't be darkened unless everyone in the family went to bed at the same time.

● When you reserve your room, ask for a cot if needed, and inquire about a babysitting service. If a hotel regularly serves families, you can have some degree of confidence in the service, as the hotel wouldn't recommend them if they received complaints. If you have any concerns, ask for references and check them.

● If you're travelling to a foreign country, tell your doctor where you're going. His/her advice will make your trip a smoother one. Also check regarding immunisations.

## Planning for a plane trip

- When possible, book seats in advance so that all family members will be together. Tell them if a non-paying infant will be sharing one of the seats. They will generally try to save a seat next to you unless the plane is 100 per cent full. When you get to the airport, remind the booking-in person that you are travelling with an infant and would like a seat held if possible.
- Check with the airline. Many have small cots for infants.
- If your child will need any medication during the trip or right after, be sure to carry it on board with you in case your bags are lost.
- Don't take milk or orange juice with you as the airline can provide them; do take apple juice.
- Select a cabin bag made of lightweight material, and choose one with lots of outside pockets for greater accessibility. You will want to pack as much as you need without overdoing it. Heavy cabin luggage is a real nuisance. Keep in mind that you may be carrying:
  - ★Nappies, plastic bags, wipes, ointment
  - ★Food
  - ★Medicine
  - ★Extra clothes, blankets, sweaters
  - ★Toys, games, books.
- Expect that there may be variations in cabin temperature so all family members should dress in layers they can add and take off as needed.

## Travel and food

- With plane travel, phone ahead to reserve a child's meal for your youngster.
- Be overprepared when it comes to food. One mother spent an additional five hours on a plane with her infant, but fortunately she was carrying enough formula to get through.
- Don't expect that the airline meal will really be your child's regular meal. If the plane is delayed, 'lunch' may be served at

4pm, so pack enough substantial food that your child can use the plane meal as entertainment, not nourishment.

- If your child is particular, take along lots of whatever you think might not be available where you are going.
- For any type of travel, food is a real help. Raisins and nuts are easy and fun.

## Travelling with older children

- Older children love the new and unexpected. Buy some activity books, games and crossword puzzles for the trip. Buy a bag with pockets and zippered compartments, and fill the pockets with different games, toys and books. Attach it to the back of the front car seat or the back of the plane seat or train seat in front of you.
- If you travel frequently, create a travel art-and-activity bag. Keep it permanently packed with paper, crayons, scissors, stickers, stars, an activity book, and mazes. It's easier than packing afresh every time, and it gives a child something specific to look forward to.
- Make tapes of records (or record your own stories). If travelling by car, you can put it on the tape deck. If travelling by plane or train, put it in a tape recorder with ear phones.
- Let your child pack his or her own *small* bag of special belongings (perhaps in an easy-to-carry backpack). A child as young as four will enjoy the importance of being able to pack for him- or herself. However, remember that you can't rely on those items to keep your child busy for the trip. You'll need to pack special items for entertainment.
- When you get to the place you're visiting, try to locate a playmate for your child. Children are rejuvenated by visits with their peers.
- Ask about local playgrounds. An hour at one can often wear off enough of a child's excess energy that the family can devote the rest of the day to sightseeing.

When I look back on my childhood, the warmest memories I have are the family trips we made. Even ten-hour car rides (and I got car-sick!) were happy times for me. So while you pack an unending supply of nappies and toys and games, just remember that it will almost certainly pay off for your family in the long run!

# INDEX